CYBERSECURITY TABLETOP EXERCISES

From Planning to Execution

by Robert Lelewski and
John Hollenberger

**no starch
press®**

San Francisco

Printed in the United States of America

First printing

28 27 26 25 24   1 2 3 4 5

ISBN-13: 978-1-7185-0382-3 (print)
ISBN-13: 978-1-7185-0383-0 (ebook)

 Published by No Starch Press®, Inc.
245 8th Street, San Francisco, CA 94103
phone: +1.415.863.9900
www.nostarch.com; info@nostarch.com

Publisher: William Pollock
Managing Editor: Jill Franklin
Production Manager: Sabrina Plomitallo-González
Production Editor: Jennifer Kepler
Developmental Editor: Frances Saux
Cover Illustrator: Rick Reese
Interior Design: Octopod Studios
Technical Reviewer: Michael Murray
Copyeditor: Rachel Monaghan
Proofreader: Ben Kot

Figure 3-5 has been reprinted courtesy of the National Institute of Standards and Technology, US Department of Commerce. Not copyrightable in the United States.

Library of Congress Control Number: 2024013020

For customer service inquiries, please contact info@nostarch.com. For information on distribution, bulk sales, corporate sales, or translations: sales@nostarch.com. For permission to translate this work: rights@nostarch.com. To report counterfeit copies or piracy: counterfeit@nostarch.com.

PRAISE FOR *CYBERSECURITY TABLETOP EXERCISES*

"This book is a great resource for anyone looking to start or enhance their cyber simulation exercise capability. The practical insights, examples, and step-by-step instructions can be immediately applied, helping readers to effectively test and evaluate a team's ability to respond to a cyber incident. Good stuff!"

—ANTHONY GIANDOMENICO, GLOBAL
VICE PRESIDENT, FORTIGUARD SECURITY
CONSULTING

"Whether you are brand new to the concept of tabletops or a seasoned professional, this book empowers both individuals and teams to learn and improve on the planning, development, and facilitation of these critical cyber exercises. *Cybersecurity Tabletop Exercises* leads readers right from the design stage through to delivery, feedback gathering, and even gaining organizational buy-in, with a variety of fabulous example scenarios and injects that many teams could simply pick up and run with! This should be on the bookshelf of any cyber professional who takes their tabletops seriously."

—REBECCA TAYLOR, THREAT INTELLIGENCE
KNOWLEDGE MANAGER, SECUREWORKS

"A must-read for anyone involved in cybersecurity incident response. It expertly covers all aspects of conducting tabletop exercises, from scenario development to delivery to evaluation, providing practical advice and examples. Get ready to design and execute impactful tabletop exercises with the help of this book!"

—JEFFREY J. CARPENTER, FIRST INCIDENT
RESPONSE HALL OF FAME INDUCTEE

"Lelewski and Hollenberger offer a masterclass in cybersecurity preparedness, covering every facet of incident response planning with meticulous detail and practical insights. Their focus on engaging an executive audience is particularly noteworthy, shedding light on the critical role that C-level executives and cross-functional leaders play in managing cybersecurity incidents. *Cybersecurity Tabletop Exercises* sets a new standard in the field and is essential reading for any organization aiming to enhance its cybersecurity readiness."

—BRIAN NESGODA, CIO/CISO, BLACK SWAN
TECHNOLOGIES

"Rob and John clearly guide readers on how to design and get the most value out of a tabletop exercise rather than it just being another compliance requirement. They will not steer you wrong!"

—TROY M. BETTENCOURT, GLOBAL PARTNER
AND HEAD OF IBM X-FORCE

For Taylor, who was willing to set off to Bolivia on what turned out to be a lifelong adventure; for Lucas, who was willing to take an intern under his wings and provide endless patient guidance; and for my dad, who set the standard.
. . . And for Beaker.

—Rob

For Jenn, who always pushes me to take a leap and ensures life is an adventure. For Cameron, Cara, Callahan, and Miguel, who bring me constant joy and love, even when I don't deserve it. For Mom and Dad, who shaped me into the person I am and who always show unconditional love. For George and David: "You go, we go." And for the countless people who have given me a chance, mentored me, and guided me throughout my career, including Jeff, Mike, Andy, and Rob. Love you all!
. . . And for Nia and Nibbler.

—John

About the Authors

Robert Lelewski has spent 20 years in the fields of information technology, digital forensics and incident response, cybersecurity, and risk management. Over his career, he has conducted hundreds of tabletop exercises and developed incident response plans for organizations across the globe, including Fortune 500 companies. He began his cybersecurity career as a computer forensic consultant, testifying on criminal and civil litigation matters, then joined IBM's incident response team. Later, he became the director of proactive services at Secureworks, where he oversaw the team's global proactive practice, helping organizations prepare for cybersecurity incidents.

Currently a vice president of cybersecurity strategy for Zurich Insurance, Robert holds several industry certifications, including the CISSP-ISSMP, CISA, CISM, CRISC, CIPM, CDPSE, and GCIH. He earned a bachelor's in economic crime investigation from Utica College of Syracuse University, a master's in technology management from the University of Denver, and an MBA from the University of Northern Iowa.

John Hollenberger has spent more than 16 years as an information security analyst and cybersecurity consultant. John began his cybersecurity journey at the CERT Coordination Center, where he coordinated and collaborated with malware analysts, incident response experts, and vulnerability analysts globally. After spending nine years in security operations, he spent several years as an IT director for a local nonprofit before moving into proactive incident response consulting with Secureworks. In his present role as a lead consultant of proactive services at Fortinet, he designs tabletop exercises and crafts incident response plans for a diverse clientele, including large corporations, small businesses, and nonprofit organizations.

Throughout his career, he has also orchestrated efficient incident response strategies, overseeing digital forensics collection, ensuring payment card industry compliance, and implementing data loss prevention measures. His qualifications include a bachelor's degree in administration of justice and an array of cybersecurity certifications, including the CISSP, CISA, CISM, CRISC, GCIH, GWAPT, and Security+.

About the Technical Reviewer

Michael Murray has spent nearly his entire career on the front lines of information security. In various positions at the CERT Coordination Center at Carnegie Mellon University's Software Engineering Institute, he focused on supporting national-level cybersecurity capabilities and improving the state of incident response and analysis operations. At Secureworks, he was a director of incident response consulting, leading a global team dedicated to helping customers prepare for and respond to cybersecurity emergencies. An active member of the information security community, Michael served on the board of directors for the Forum of Incident Response and Security Teams and is currently a senior security architect for Sheetz, Inc.

BRIEF CONTENTS

CONTENTS IN DETAIL

4
FACILITATING A SUCCESSFUL TABLETOP EXERCISE   83

5
ACTING ON WHAT YOU'VE LEARNED: EVALUATION
AND NEXT STEPS   103

PART II: EXAMPLE SCENARIOS 117

6
ENGAGING A TECHNICAL AUDIENCE 119

7
ENGAGING AN EXECUTIVE AUDIENCE 135

8
ENGAGING THE BUSINESS 145

ACKNOWLEDGMENTS

We would like to thank No Starch Press's Bill Pollock for entertaining a book proposal from two untested authors and Frances Saux for spending countless hours reading drafts, providing feedback, and finding ways to balance different perspectives on how to create this book.

We're grateful to everyone who supported this endeavor, whether by enabling us to spend an hour or two writing between obligations or providing feedback on initial ideas. Thank you.

Finally, we would be remiss if we didn't acknowledge those who were willing to share their knowledge with us throughout our careers. Countless individuals, including managers, peers, and clients, took the time to offer constructive criticism and helped us grow our craft.

INTRODUCTION

Nearly every day, we receive calls from clients who tell us things like "The board asked us to perform a tabletop exercise by the end of the year" or "Our auditors want us to test our incident response process, and we don't know how."

Chances are, if you've picked up this book, you, too, have been tasked with helping your organization prepare for a future cybersecurity incident, perhaps through the use of a tabletop exercise. In a *tabletop exercise*, members of an organization gather to discuss how they would respond to a potential future event or emergency. We'll dive into the specific characteristics of cybersecurity tabletop exercises in more detail in Chapter 1, but in brief, most contain the following features:

- They're usually purely discussion-based exercises. This sets them apart from red-teaming drills or other operations-based exercises, which require hands-on activities.
- They focus on exploring a specific scenario, such as a past event or a hypothetical incident inspired by plausible risks to the organization.

- They gather participants in a low-stress environment that emphasizes collaboration and the identification of deficiencies. To that end, they're designed to encourage participation and solicit feedback.

- They enable participants to evaluate the organization's decision-making process, as well as its existing procedures and documentation. They also let participants discuss their individual roles and respective functional interests during a potential incident.

While such an exercise might seem straightforward, every organization is unique, with its own culture, regulatory environment, industry vertical, and risk landscape. To have maximum value, the exercise must consider and accommodate the organization's unique needs.

We wrote this book based on our experience delivering hundreds of tabletop exercises as consultants for numerous types of organizations, including nonprofits, manufacturing firms, regional banks, utility companies, educational institutions, and governments at various levels. In it, you'll find examples of tabletop exercises suited to different purposes, as well as detailed guidance on how to plan, facilitate, and learn from them. The considerations we discuss herein should help you make your tabletop exercise process smoother and deliver the greatest benefit to your organization.

Who Should Read This Book and Why

This book has several audiences in mind. The first is information security professionals and those in related roles who are tasked with creating and facilitating a tabletop exercise for their employer. These individuals might need help executing their organization's first tabletop exercise, or they might want to improve their performance in an ongoing series of exercises. Moreover, the people tasked with developing these exercises most likely have other job responsibilities, so in many organizations, it is difficult to perform a tabletop exercise more than once a year, and those overseeing them may have little opportunity to become experts in the topic.

We also target information security consultants who serve as external resources for other organizations seeking to perform a tabletop exercise. Companies that provide information security services frequently receive requests for help creating and facilitating a tabletop exercise. Given our extensive background in information security consulting, we would be remiss if we didn't include the lessons we've learned from the consulting side.

Finally, while we've approached the book with information security in mind, you could adapt much of the process we discuss to other facets of the organization. Non–information security exercises might evaluate the organization's readiness for business continuity issues (such as the impact of a sustained power outage at an assisted care facility) or physical security events, for example.

What's in This Book

This book is split into two sections. Part I provides guidance on how to plan and execute a tabletop exercise, while Part II contains sample exercise scenarios that you could leverage for your own events, along with suggestions for adapting them.

Part I is organized linearly. It begins by discussing why you might want to pursue a tabletop exercise in the first place, then covers the planning and scenario development steps, techniques for successfully facilitating the exercise, and ways to evaluate the event's success.

Chapter 1, Why Perform Tabletop Exercises?   In some organizations, you'll need to create the business case for performing a tabletop exercise, and this chapter will help bolster your argument. We'll explore how tabletop exercises can help an organization align with standards, practice for the inevitable bad day, evaluate the policy implications of a cybersecurity incident, examine technical controls, and identify process deficiencies.

Chapter 2, Planning the Tabletop Exercise   This chapter contains many of the foundational activities that need to occur well before the tabletop exercise itself. These involve defining goals and objectives, determining whom to invite, addressing logistical concerns, and crafting a robust and multifaceted communications plan to engage all stakeholders.

Chapter 3, The Development Process: Where the Rubber Meets the Road   With the key planning tasks complete, you can now develop the tabletop exercise. This chapter outlines the steps for constructing the tabletop exercise, including selecting a scenario and breaking it down into logical injects—a set of new or clarifying facts about the scenario—that force attendees to respond to events with limited information. This chapter also discusses how to create the presentation deck.

Chapter 4, Facilitating a Successful Tabletop Exercise   For some, facilitating a tabletop exercise can seem daunting. You might find it intimidating to speak in front of your colleagues (some of whom you might be meeting for the first time) to discuss the actions they would take during a crisis. This chapter will provide tips for successfully delivering a tabletop exercise, encouraging group participation, and making the discussion as valuable as possible.

Chapter 5, Acting on What You've Learned: Evaluation and Next Steps   After you've completed the tabletop exercise, it's time to evaluate your successes and identify opportunities for improvement. This chapter covers how to review the lessons learned from the exercise and develop an action plan to remedy shortcomings. We'll also discuss strategies for maintaining your momentum to ensure the tabletop doesn't become a one-off, check-the-box affair.

Part II contains examples of tabletop exercises designed for technical and executive audiences, as well as other roles in an organization. These examples can serve as inspiration for those seeking to perform their own tabletop exercises. For each exercise sample, we offer possible modifications that should help you adapt the scenario to your organization's particular needs.

Chapter 6, Engaging a Technical Audience   These tabletop exercises are excellent options to present to a technical audience, as they hit on many of the common technical questions that emerge during incident response efforts. The scenarios include phishing, ransomware, a zero-day vulnerability, and a supply chain compromise.

Chapter 7, Engaging an Executive Audience   The scenarios in this chapter incorporate many of the issues that are important for an executive audience to consider. We consider the managerial aspects of a ransomware response, the discovery of sensitive data on the dark web, and distributed denial-of-service attacks.

Chapter 8, Engaging the Business   It's often important for a tabletop exercise to include other teams in an organization, such as human resources and physical security. The scenarios in this chapter cover a physical security breach, a social media compromise, and an insider threat.

The appendix contains helpful report templates, which can be used to show internal and external stakeholders that a tabletop exercise was performed and provide details of the scenario exercises as well as findings or observations that were uncovered. Throughout the book, you'll find case studies discussing tabletops that went according to plan—and, occasionally, ones that went awry. We've included these examples so that you can learn from the efforts of others. While we've fictionalized these stories and the names of the organizations involved, the events are based on actual engagements we've undertaken in our careers.

The Book's Scope

The security community widely considers tabletop exercises a necessity to reduce the risks an organization faces. For this reason, many authorities—including the US Department of Homeland Security, the International Organization for Standardization, the French National Agency for the Security of Information Systems, and the National Institute of Standards and Technology—have released guidelines on preparing for disasters using tabletop exercises.

These agencies have similar definitions and processes for performing security exercises. For consistency, however, this book uses those created by the United States' Homeland Security Exercise and Evaluation Program (HSEEP), which defines an exercise as "an event or activity, delivered through discussion or action, to develop, assess, or validate plans, policies, procedures, and capabilities that jurisdictions/organizations can use to achieve planned outcomes."

A subset of the previously defined exercise includes discussion-based exercises, which would include tabletop exercises, as well as seminars, workshops, and games. According to HSEEP, discussion-based exercises tend to include teams new to incident response, or teams that want to become acquainted with new plans, procedures, or other team members. Nevertheless, mature teams should not discount the value of discussion-based exercises. These exercises are usually led by facilitators and constrained by a shorter execution window (for example, two hours). While HSEEP states that discussion-based exercises tend to focus on "strategic, policy-oriented" issues, they can just as easily include technical discussions.

One final note on the book's scope: we've spent most of our careers working in North America and Europe. As a result, the standards and practices we discuss come from agencies in these regions. If you're performing tabletop exercises elsewhere, consider the advice of the industry authorities in your area to supplement the discussions in this book.

PART I

THE TABLETOP EXERCISE PROCESS

In Chapters 1 through 5, we will guide you through the tabletop exercise development process. This includes exploring the importance of tabletop exercises, the planning and development process, facilitation strategies, evaluation techniques, and steps to perform after the conclusion of your successful tabletop exercise. While every effort has been made to provide universally applicable guidance, you may need to provide minor alterations in order to align with your organization's processes and cultural norms.

1

WHY PERFORM TABLETOP EXERCISES?

Organizations and individuals performed tabletop exercises well before computers were invented. It isn't hard to imagine that military generals of the past conducted them to discuss hypothetical attacks, troop movements, and defenses. More recently, tabletop exercises have prepared people for pandemics, natural disasters, nuclear accidents, oil spills, and other events that require a significant response and the coordination of disparate resources.

Only recently have tabletop exercises expanded to include cybersecurity events. Broadly, a *cybersecurity tabletop exercise* is a conversation between those responsible for fulfilling a variety of roles during a cybersecurity incident. In the exercise, the participants, representing a range of organizational interests, walk through a hypothetical scenario and discuss how they would respond to it. With the right planning, cybersecurity tabletop exercises can be an effective, engaging, and relatively low-cost way to prepare an organization's information assurance program for the inevitable cybersecurity incident. In this chapter, we consider why an organization might choose to conduct a tabletop exercise, how it can benefit from doing so, and what advantages these exercises have over other approaches.

Reasons to Conduct a Tabletop Exercise

The benefits of a tabletop exercise to an organization's security culture and business can vary based on its maturity. This section outlines possible benefits, ranging from small to significant.

Improve Incident Response Team Collaboration

All incident response teams have to start somewhere. Some organizations conduct tabletop exercises merely to assemble team members in one room so they can get to know each other, discuss their individual interests, and forge relationships. Here are a few basic scenarios where this might be the case:

- Because of recent staff turnover, employees are unfamiliar with each other and their roles.
- Due to recently implemented regulatory standards, several people have been newly assigned a role in the incident response process.
- The organization has recently formalized an incident response team, and some people on it have never participated in an incident.
- After a merger or acquisition, groups of employees with different systems and processes must come together to address a cybersecurity incident.
- The increasing complexity of incidents has required nontechnical employees (in fields such as legal, compliance, and human resources) to consider how they would respond to a cybersecurity incident.
- The organization has introduced new technology or business processes that may impact how the team responds to a cybersecurity incident.

When stakeholders gather to discuss the incident response process, they can understand their respective priorities, share their plans, and build momentum for future initiatives. In some workplaces, participants may already have strong bonds; however, it's not uncommon for many to be meeting each other for the first time during the tabletop exercise.

Clarify Team Roles and Responsibilities

Gone are the days in which a cybersecurity event is a one-person operation. Today, incident response requires input from various stakeholders from both technical and strategic backgrounds. Consider how many parties may respond in the basic case of an HR employee clicking a phishing email attachment that downloads malware:

Information security manager   Leads the investigatory efforts and reports to management, if necessary

Information security analyst   Performs basic forensic and malware analysis to determine what files were impacted on the HR system

Network administrator   Examines relevant logs from network ingress and egress points to identify suspicious activity

Human resources manager   Initiates potential disciplinary actions against the employee who compromised the environment and presumably broke a policy

Legal   Determines whether external notifications to governmental authorities or third-party entities are required based on the files that were accessed by the malware

Risk management   Assesses whether the organization must perform corrective actions to protect itself in the future

Chief information security officer (CISO)   Notifies the organization's C level, provides status reports, and gives a final disposition; conveys the incident's impact on the organization's priorities

With so many people involved in the response, it's important that everyone understands their specific roles and responsibilities from the first moments of an event to avoid wasting precious time determining who should do what. This involves adhering to the chain of command and established communication protocols. Tabletop exercises provide an environment that allows the team to clarify who is part of the response process and what their responsibilities are.

Assess the Impact of Process Changes

All organizations, from nonprofits to tech companies, evolve for a multitude of reasons: laws and regulations are introduced or amended; new competitors emerge; tools and techniques are developed. It's important to consider the impact of these changes on the organization's overall risk.

Tabletop exercises are an excellent opportunity to explore process changes and their potential impact on incident response. Some of these process changes may be mundane; for example, after implementing a new ticketing system, the incident response team should verify that the help desk can identify a cybersecurity incident and promptly escalate the incident ticket to the right person. Other process changes may be larger in scale, such as the acquisition of a new business unit, in which case the incident response team should ensure its response process aligns with the workings of the new business unit.

After a process change, an organization could use a tabletop to explore unexpected impacts on the incident response team's ability to perform its duties or to confirm that the change does not affect its incident response process.

Finally, for the forward-thinking organization, a tabletop exercise can explore the effect of a proposed process change *before* it is implemented. Discovering a potentially unwanted impact early enables the organization to make changes before implementing the new process, when alterations are less costly.

CASE STUDY: RESPONDING TO NEW LAWS

Neptune Pharma, a pharmaceutical manufacturer based in Pittsburgh, Pennsylvania, performed its manufacturing in Barbados, where 150 of its employees were based. In 2019, in response to Europe's General Data Protection Regulation (GDPR), Barbados passed the Data Protection Act, which regulates the collection, processing, and dissemination of personal data.

Due to its business interests in Barbados, Neptune Pharma had tracked the new legislation and adjusted company policies to comply with it. Now the company's CISO was requesting a tabletop exercise with information security personnel and legal counsels in both the United States and Barbados. While the CISO didn't have specific cause for concern, he knew from experience that data privacy legislation had the potential to impact incident response efforts.

Worried about corporate espionage, Neptune Pharma focused the tabletop on an insider threat scenario; the company manufactured drugs that represented decades of research and large financial investments, which could all be compromised with a simple $100,000 bribe to the right employee. The tabletop exercise scenario was relatively simple: Neptune Pharma believed an employee was selling sensitive pharmaceutical products to a foreign competitor.

During the tabletop, the corporate security team said they wanted to investigate the suspected employee's work computer and mobile phone by shipping the devices to their corporate headquarters in the United States. Shipping devices was standard practice, as the forensic lab was located in Pittsburgh. But the Barbadian legal counsel brought up concerns: if the devices contained employee personal data (including salary information), sending the devices outside Barbados would violate the new Data Protection Act.

The tabletop exercise had discovered a gap in Neptune Pharma's incident response process. While the company would have probably implemented a workaround during an incident, such as sending Neptune Pharma's corporate investigators to Barbados to perform the analysis, it could now remedy the issue well before any incident occurred.

Reduce the Cost of Data Breaches

Gaining management support for information security initiatives often requires connecting the initiative to business considerations. Fortunately, there is quantifiable financial value in performing a tabletop exercise; in their *Cost of a Data Breach* reports, the Ponemon Institute and IBM Security have consistently demonstrated that incident response exercises provide significant savings in the case of a data breach, as shown in Table 1-1.

Table 1-1: Average Cost of a Data Breach in Millions

Type of security preparation	Cost of breach with a high level of preparation	Cost of breach with a low level of preparation
DevSecOps	$3.54	$5.22
Incident response plan and testing	$3.62	$5.11
Employee training	$3.68	$5.18

Source: Ponemon Institute and IBM Security, *Cost of a Data Breach Report 2023* (Armonk, NY: IBM Corporation, 2023).

The 2023 report found that having an incident response plan and testing it regularly is the second most impactful cost mitigator of 28 studied factors. The difference can be staggering: organizations with high levels of incident response planning and testing have an average breach cost of $3.62 million, compared to $5.11 million for those with little to none.

Furthermore, organizations that test their incident response plans benefit from being able to identify and contain an incident faster—and thus get back to business more quickly—than those that do not (Table 1-2).

Table 1-2: Time Needed to Identify and Contain a Data Breach

Maturity level	Mean time to identify	Mean time to contain	Total time
Organization has no incident response team and has not conducted incident response plan testing	216 days	90 days	306 days
Organization has an incident response team	208 days	80 days	288 days
Organization has conducted incident response plan testing	196 days	62 days	258 days
Organization has an incident response team and has conducted incident response plan testing	194 days	58 days	252 days

Source: Ponemon Institute and IBM Security, *Cost of a Data Breach Report 2023* (Armonk, NY: IBM Corporation, 2023).

Organizations that test their incident response plan have a mean time to identify of 196 days and a mean time to contain of 62 days, which is faster than organizations that just have an incident response team.

Note that the 2023 report focuses on data breaches in which data was lost or stolen, which are just a subset of cybersecurity incidents. Furthermore, the data combines incident response planning and testing, and the organization could have used various testing methods; for example, it may have leveraged hands-on adversarial testing teams (so-called red teams) or performed less intensive tabletop exercises. Even so, the findings suggest that a tabletop exercise (one form of testing) can act as a mitigating control, decreasing the overall financial impact of a breach on the organization.

Improve Security Awareness

All employees should be able to identify a threat and escalate it to the proper channels. There are many ways to develop a culture of security awareness across a workforce, ranging from mundane to creative. A client once told us, "My best investment in information security? It's most certainly not a fancy tool. I have a line item in my budget that, every year, I need to fight to keep in: $10,000 for gift cards to the coffee shop in the lobby." Whenever a team member did something right, whether it was keeping their desk clean at night, asking a tailgater at the entrance to scan their badge, or properly responding to a phishing email, the client dropped a $10 gift card on the team member's desk with a note thanking them for their action. The team member typically proceeded to gleefully tell colleagues about the gift card, amplifying the effect of the initiative.

Tabletop exercises are another method to increase security awareness in the organization. Attendees can learn how to identify a threat and take a desired action (such as notifying the information security manager). They can also learn the implications of *not* taking the correct action, which is particularly valuable for participants coming from outside the cybersecurity realm.

Tabletop exercises are generally a more engaging form of security training than, say, a prerecorded video (though maybe not as exciting as free coffee!), and they can be tailored to a very specific audience, such as people with important positions at the company or those with a track record of poor security hygiene.

CASE STUDY: FOSTERING SECURITY AWARENESS

Pacific Northwest Hospital (PNH) found itself the continual victim of phishing attacks. Much to the frustration of its security team, an estimated half of these incidents stemmed from end users clicking links contained in phishing email. The resulting damage ranged from relatively minor issues like streams of pop-up advertisements to more severe situations involving the introduction of ransomware.

To tackle the issue, PNH's risk management team launched a user education campaign that included training employees, sending them regular test phishing email messages, rewarding them for taking the correct action, and even subjecting them to unorthodox, attention-getting stunts (like hiring someone to lurk around the lobby wearing an oversized fish costume and handing out business cards reading "Click me").

To complement the educational campaign, the information security director conducted two tabletop exercises, one for technical members and another for executive members of the incident response team. Both exercises used phishing as the threat vector. Because the audience was already aware of the perils of phishing, they participated more than usual and didn't need to be convinced that the scenario was plausible and deserved their attention.

If a tabletop exercise had been the only conduit for raising awareness of phishing email, PNH might have had limited success in changing its dismal phishing numbers. But in concert with other awareness efforts, the tabletop exercise solidified participants' understanding of the risk.

Explore Key Questions

During a cybersecurity incident, the organization will inevitably be faced with key questions at various points throughout the incident response process. Some of these questions are trivial, while others may have an outsized impact on the organization's ability to respond. A tabletop exercise enables a group to discuss and iron out questions like the following outside an emergency situation:

- Who needs to be involved in the process?
- Who needs to be notified, internally and externally?
- What do we need to add or change in the incident response plan or playbooks?
- What are our weakest links?
- When do regulators or cyber insurance carriers need to be notified?
- Do contractual obligations require us to notify other business entities?
- When do we need to escalate the incident?
- Where is the critical data and system?

Prepare Senior Leadership for an Incident

Today, senior leadership and the board of directors are often asking if an organization is ready for a cybersecurity incident. One of the most significant reasons for this is the increased attention from regulatory authorities, especially those overseeing publicly traded entities. Guidance from the US Securities and Exchange Commission (SEC), which regulates publicly traded companies in the United States, encourages public disclosures detailing the risks of cybersecurity incidents.

Keeping investors informed of cybersecurity risks is now a standard disclosure data point in a Form 10-K, an annual report required by the SEC to provide insight into the organization's finances. The majority of the board of directors must sign 10-K reports, and senior leadership plays a significant role in preparing their documentation. In a 2018 study titled "Examining Cybersecurity Risk Reporting on US SEC Form 10-K" (*https://www.isaca.org/ resources/isaca-journal/issues/2018/volume-5/examining-cybersecurity-risk-reporting -on-us-sec-form-10-k*), CPA Grace Johnson found that cybersecurity risk was listed in the 10-Ks of all corporations included in her research, more companies were providing cybersecurity risk information, and 40 percent of the risk disclosures were "detailed and specific."

Tabletop exercises are one avenue for ensuring that boards and senior leadership are properly prepared for a cybersecurity incident.

Align with Industry Standards

Many organizations must follow industry standards and best practices, some of which specifically require testing incident response plans. For some businesses, complying with frameworks is a legal requirement, while others choose to follow them to communicate their commitment to cyber-security. Newer organizations might aspire to meet these standards as they grow and mature. In each case, aligning organizational information security initiatives with standards ensures that they are grounded in a solid foundation.

The International Organization for Standardization (ISO), the National Institute of Standards and Technology (NIST), the Center for Internet Security (CIS), and the Defense Federal Acquisition Regulation Supplement (DFARS) all recommend conducting preparatory activities, such as tabletop exercises:

ISO/IEC 27001: *Information Security, Cybersecurity, and Privacy Protection— Information Security Management Systems—Requirements*

> ISO/IEC 27001 is a well-known international standard that focuses on information security management. This standard recommends that organizations have a well-maintained and tested incident response plan; in section A.16, it stipulates that organizations should handle inci-dents consistently and have a process in place by which to learn from incidents. Organizations can rehearse their plans through tabletop exercises to align with ISO/IEC 27001.

NIST Special Publication 800-84: *Guide to Test, Training, and Exercise Programs for IT Plans and Capabilities*

> For organizations that turn to NIST for guidance, look no further than NIST Special Publication (SP) 800-84. This exceptional publication recommends developing a testing, training, and exercise program and has specific sections that focus on tabletop exercises, functional exer-cises, and tests, all of which help improve the organization's incident response capabilities. While the remaining chapters of this book will touch on the key concepts of the incident response process, we recom-mend that readers review this publication at *https://csrc.nist.gov/pubs/sp/ 800/84/final.*

Center for Internet Security

CIS releases a list of critical security controls that organizations can implement to protect themselves from cyberattacks. Many organizations follow CIS to enhance their security posture. If your organization does so, it would be worth reviewing Control 17 and, more specifically, section 17.7, which recommends that organizations "plan and conduct routine incident response exercises . . . on an annual basis." While the controls do not specifically indicate that the incident response exercise is a tabletop, CIS has released numerous tabletop exercise templates; search for "tabletop exercises" at *https://www.cisecurity.org*.

Defense Federal Acquisition Regulation Supplement

In 2015, the US Department of Defense (DoD) published DFARS to protect controlled but unclassified information. DFARS is more of a contract requirement than a standard and is required for any organization that performs business with the DoD. The necessary controls can be found in NIST SP 800-171: *Protecting Controlled Unclassified Information in Nonfederal Systems and Organizations*. Of note, section 3.6.3 lists tabletop exercises as one means of testing the effectiveness of an organization's incident response.

Fulfill Contractual Requirements

Increasingly, organizations that do business with each other must examine how these business interactions impact their overall cybersecurity risk. Often, one organization grants another limited access to a system so it can perform some service. For example, a manufacturing organization may give a vendor remote access to key manufacturing systems so that the vendor can perform software updates on them. Thus, if a threat actor were to compromise one party in the relationship, the other party that shares system access might also be impacted.

Because of this risk, organizations may insert language into their contracts defining minimum information security standards as well as requirements of either party in the event of a security incident. The contract might require an organization to perform regular tests of an incident response process, including a tabletop exercise. DFARS, mentioned in the previous section, is one example of a contractual requirement that organizations must adhere to if performing services for the DoD.

Another example is the Payment Card Industry Data Security Standard (PCI-DSS), an information security standard required by various credit card brands. PCI-DSS requires merchants who process credit cards to adhere to a set of information security controls designed to minimize the risk posed to the credit card brand. The standard requires that organizations test their incident response plan at least annually.

The tabletop exercise should not, however, become a "check the box" affair item to fulfill a contractual obligation or a regulatory requirement. Attendees should all understand that the tabletop exercise is an opportunity to learn, grow, and prepare for a cybersecurity emergency.

Examine a Recent Cybersecurity Incident

A tabletop exercise based on a recent cybersecurity incident may be an extension of the *lessons learned* stage of the incident response process. This stage can range from hosting an informal discussion to making a formal report and debriefing executive leadership. A tabletop exercise could supplement preexisting lessons learned activities and provide value even if performed several months after the incident.

A "recent cybersecurity incident" doesn't have to mean a catastrophic event that put the organization into a tailspin. Instead, these examinations could explore a simpler incident, such as a well-placed spam email that a user clicked, or an employee installing and using nonapproved cloud storage software to save sensitive information, thereby violating the organization's data practices. These basic incidents may be just as valuable to examine as an incident involving nation-state actors, silent reconnaissance, or a highly advanced piece of zero-day malware.

Because the organization has more context on how an incident occurred, the exercise facilitator could discuss what prompted the user to install the software in the first place (such as a lack of awareness) or whether current security controls are adequate to detect and prevent a similar incident. Cross-functional issues, such as the role of the HR or legal teams, are other notable avenues of exploration.

Finally, when a tabletop exercise scenario is based on what has *actually* happened versus what *could* happen, there's often a greater level of collaboration among participants. They sometimes hesitate to completely buy into a tabletop scenario, thinking, *Could this really happen to us?*, but a cybersecurity incident that really did occur requires no suspension of disbelief.

Identify and Prioritize Risks

Organizations might also want to perform tabletop exercises to rehearse various risk scenarios that may affect them. Of course, in order to do so, they must first understand what the top risks are. It's helpful to have a *risk register*, a tool that identifies and categorizes each risk to the organization and includes information like type of risk, description, probability, priority, and mitigation response.

Included in this risk register should be risks that could affect the confidentiality, availability, or integrity of the organization's data. These might include ransomware, malware, denial of service, lost or stolen laptops, business email compromise, and credential theft, among others. If you're unsure of the risks affecting your organization, consider networking with industry peers and reviewing current threats to your industry vertical. Risks affecting a health system will be very different from those affecting a manufacturing plant.

With risks defined, you can then select one (or more) to focus on during the tabletop exercise. Approaches to selecting a risk may vary; some teams prioritize the highest risk to the organization, while others spend time exploring unfamiliar threats or risks that represent the technical team's largest weakness. Next, include the appropriate team members in the exercise; we'll offer guidance on this step in Chapter 2.

Tabletop exercises can also uncover new risks to the organization. Any new risks should be properly documented, reviewed, and prioritized during the evaluation stage of the exercise (discussed in Chapter 5).

Advantages of Tabletops over Other Security Exercises

Tabletop exercises are just one way to train staff, assess residual risk after an incident, and refine processes. An organization could also hire red teams to actively probe systems for vulnerabilities or perform classroom-oriented security awareness training, for example. But tabletop exercises do provide a few advantages over other training and testing formats.

Low Cost and High Return on Investment

Tabletop exercises are an extremely cost-effective way to explore an organization's plans, policies, and procedures. Additionally, they ensure that employees understand the processes they must follow in the event of a cybersecurity incident. Unlike some security exercises (for example, red teaming), a tabletop exercise requires no additional equipment beyond the standard office suite of tools, a conference room, and a projector. You won't need technical resources the way you would in a hands-on exercise, only employees' time.

Even with its low overhead, the return on investment from a tabletop exercise can be significant. Consider the value of these lessons learned from tabletop exercises:

- In discussing a scenario involving the compromise of social media accounts, you discover that the social media accounts followed by thousands of customers use a password shared by multiple employees and lack multifactor authentication: two compounding security failures.

- During a ransomware-themed tabletop exercise in which the organization decides to pay a ransom, you determine that the organization lacks a method to quickly attain and transfer cryptocurrency. This step alone could add several hours or days to the process, prolonging the incident.

- When discussing how the information security team would analyze a suspicious employee's laptop during an employee misconduct scenario, staff determines that they lack common computer forensic tools needed to preserve the employee's hard drive.

If discovered by a low-cost tabletop exercise and rectified, each of these process deficiencies could mitigate a costly cybersecurity incident or lead to a swifter resolution.

Finally, high-quality tabletop exercise templates are increasingly available for no cost from a variety of reputable sources. The US-based CISA (the Cybersecurity and Infrastructure Security Agency) is just one of many sources that provide free tabletop exercise templates for organizations wishing to conduct their own internal tabletop exercises (*https://www.cisa.gov/cisa-tabletop-exercise-packages*). We discuss other sources in Chapter 3.

Efficiency

Tabletop exercises offer an additional perk: they let you discuss an incident, from identification to remediation, in a matter of hours. By contrast, operations-based exercises require staff to respond to activities in real time, such as by performing containment measures (like severing network connectivity) and conducting analysis (like investigating logs and artifacts).

According to the European Union Agency for Cybersecurity (better known as ENISA), it takes approximately 206 days to detect a data breach. (You can find its report, titled "ENISA Threat Landscape 2020 - Data Breach," at *https://www.enisa.europa.eu/publications/enisa-threat-landscape-2020-data-breach*.) This is in line with the Ponemon Institute and IBM Security's finding that, in 2023, it took an average of 204 days to identify a data breach and another 73 days to contain it. A tabletop exercise takes an event that would normally require significant time to identify—and even more time to resolve—and compresses the discussion down to a few hours. When a discussion point is brought up that may require hours or days of work, the facilitator of the exercise can artificially "move the clock ahead" and provide the next block of information to consider, filling in any information gaps. We discuss these strategies further in Chapter 3.

Tabletop exercises are a compromise to balance the time an employee spends preparing for events and performing their primary job. Requiring key personnel to plan an operations-based exercise and then devote one or more working days to play out the response may not be tenable for many organizations.

No Operational Disruption

Every business has information systems that are key to its operations—for example, medical equipment that monitors patient health, manufacturing equipment whose downtime would result in significant financial loss, and operational technology that controls banks of elevators in a high-rise building.

An obvious benefit of tabletop exercises is that they don't require interacting with critical systems in a way that could impact human safety or cause serious financial harm to the organization. On the other hand, even very basic operations-based exercises would involve interacting with critical information systems. In some cases, this might be too risky or downright irresponsible.

Tabletop exercises enable experts on critical systems to discuss hypothetical cybersecurity incidents without actually interacting with those systems. This discussion allows them to better identify weaknesses that may cause a cybersecurity incident, potential containment and analysis strategies, and the implications of an incident.

**CASE STUDY: SAFELY TESTING
MANUFACTURING SYSTEMS**

The new director of information security at Pacific Baby Formula, a nutrition company that makes infant formulas, wanted to test the organization's ability to respond to a security event involving its manufacturing systems. However, the chief risk officer informed him that they couldn't perform penetration tests on the manufacturing lines due to strict quality controls and safety concerns.

He struck a compromise: instead of actively testing the manufacturing infrastructure, he used a tabletop exercise to explore how a cybersecurity incident involving those systems might play out. The premise of the exercise was that a contractor had accidentally introduced malware into the environment while servicing those systems. The malware, which was nothing more than a cryptocurrency miner, impacted multiple manufacturing systems by consuming processing power. To contain the incident, parts of the manufacturing pipeline were shut down.

The tabletop exercise revealed several deficiencies in the company's ability to identify and respond to a cybersecurity incident:

- Several operational technology devices weren't monitored for potentially malicious software.

- IT contractors regularly updated the software for certain specialty manufacturing equipment, and the process of verifying IT contractors' software patches had gaps that would have allowed malicious software to enter the environment.

- The team maintaining the manufacturing plant operations would not have notified the information security team in a timely manner because the teams had different standards for what constituted a security incident.

- If impacted by malware, certain manufacturing systems would have taken days to service, creating an unacceptable period of downtime.

Each of these issues had the potential to cause a cybersecurity incident or stifle its response; if combined, they could be catastrophic. Even without hands-on testing, the tabletop yielded significant findings.

What Tabletop Exercises Can Test

Because tabletop exercises require minimal infrastructure, there are few limitations to what they can test. In discussion-based exercises, you might begin by focusing on technical controls, only for other issues (such as problems with a vendor contract) to emerge as a focal point. Even so, organizations often find it beneficial to narrow their focus by digging deep into one topic or focusing on organizational goals (such as reducing risk to a critical system). This section will review a number of common focus areas.

The Potential Impact of Current Threats

You can use tabletop exercises to continually explore the cybersecurity threat landscape and how it applies to your organization. It's no secret that the threat landscape evolves frequently—consider just a few events over the past several decades:

The Morris Worm (1988)

> This self-replicating piece of code created by Robert Morris caused the early internet to come crashing to a halt, highlighting the vulnerabilities of information systems.

Distributed denial-of-service (DDoS) attacks (2000)

> Fifteen-year-old Michael Calce managed to take several websites offline, including Yahoo!, Amazon.com, and eBay, causing cyberattacks to enter the mainstream conversation.

Stuxnet (2010)

> This worm, which targeted Iranian centrifuges responsible for enriching uranium, was believed to be a cyberweapon for possible use in a nuclear attack.

The Shamoon virus (2012)

> Designed to cause destruction in victim networks by erasing operating systems, this virus greatly impacted Saudi Arabia's state-owned oil company, Saudi Aramco.

Sony Pictures' film *The Interview* **(2014)**

> Angered by this film's portrayal of North Korean leader Kim Jong Un, the North Korea–connected hacker group Guardians of Peace attacked Sony, stealing and then releasing significant personal information and intellectual property in an attempt to harm the company.

Colonial Pipeline ransomware attack (2021)

> This event shut down Colonial Pipeline, which transports almost half the fuel on the East Coast of the United States, causing widespread fuel shortages. Ransomware is the number one threat identified by ENISA for that reporting period and has been a significant concern for the better part of a decade.

Casino hacks (2023)

> This series of cyberattacks leveraged social engineering and other techniques to cause havoc for the Caesars and MGM casinos. According to an MGM Resorts International regulatory filing, it caused an approximate loss of $100 million due to interruptions in revenue, remediation efforts, and other factors.

As highlighted in these examples, the threat landscape has evolved from relatively simple attacks impacting availability to more purposeful attacks aimed at stealing intellectual property or for financial gain. Threat landscapes change because threat actors—whether individuals, groups, or nation-states—have unique motivations that also evolve. Factors completely independent of traditional cybersecurity, such as the emergence of new attack vectors or geopolitical issues, can also change the threat landscape, as was the case during the COVID-19 pandemic when many workforces adjusted to working from home.

By performing exercises that take into account the current threat landscape or plausible hypothetical scenarios, organizations can assess whether they have properly prioritized their security investments. For example, an organization involved in critical infrastructure (such as water and electric distribution) would take particular interest in the Colonial Pipeline attack, knowing that attackers recently targeted critical infrastructure. Also, because organizations can perform simplified tabletop exercises on an ad hoc basis with minimal planning, they can relatively easily tailor an exercise topic to a recent news event to assess its impact on the organization.

**CASE STUDY: AN AD HOC RESPONSE
TO CURRENT EVENTS**

Canadian Shield Bank, a regional financial institution in Ontario, Canada, became aware of a spike in smishing attacks targeting the banking industry. *Smishing* is a type of phishing attack that attempts to trick mobile phone users into clicking links sent via SMS. A regional competitor had reported a large number of these texts, which claimed that the victims' checking accounts were overdrawn and prompted them to click a link to avoid overdraft fees.

To supplement its mandated yearly tabletop exercises, Canadian Shield Bank ran an ad hoc tabletop: a quick one-hour discussion over lunch to play out how such an attack would impact the company and what response steps might be required. By all accounts, the tabletop exercise succeeded: Canadian Shield Bank identified a number of process improvements and gaps it had not previously considered, as this was the first time its region had seen such attacks. For example, participants realized they didn't have a method to quickly warn bank customers via the bank app or text messaging.

Going forward, the bank began performing short quarterly tabletop exercises based on changes to the threat landscape and within one week of a unique threat popping up on its radar. Because the tabletop exercise scenarios weren't based on a hypothetical "what if?" and took few creative liberties, participants were far more likely to think critically about how the incident would play out at the company.

The Sufficiency of the Information Security Budget

When information security teams want to implement a certain technology, develop a product, or add head count to the team, they usually must make a business case for the added cost. One way to use tabletop exercises is to explore an already known risk in an effort to raise awareness of it and form a coalition that supports dedicating resources to mitigating it.

For example, if an information security manager recognizes that the current budget to maintain and store logs is inadequate, the tabletop can weave in a component that highlights the logging deficiency and its potential impact on a cybersecurity incident. This strategy may work best if the exercise uses an external facilitator to point out the deficiency, as the information security manager may be perceived as biased.

Tabletop exercises are an excellent way to highlight current gaps in the environment because they are flexible and can be built around a known deficiency. The exercise provides a forum for the information security team to demonstrate why an investment is needed and what the costs of inaction would be.

Information Sharing Protocols for IoCs

When responding to an event, the team might want or feel obligated to share *indicators of compromise (IoCs)* with other entities. IoCs are artifacts unique to the cybersecurity incident that are identified on devices in the organization's network and, if observed elsewhere (either internally or in another organization), may indicate the further spread of a cybersecurity incident. IoCs could include firewall logs showing that a system beaconed out to a suspicious network address, unique registry changes on an operating system, or characteristics of possible malicious files.

IoCs are extremely valuable, as they may be the first digital breadcrumbs available to identify how far an incident has spread. Some organizations are contractually obligated to share these details, or they may do so for altruistic reasons to allow potentially affected entities to bolster their own defenses against a mutual cyber adversary.

Tabletop exercises are an excellent way to discuss how to share information with outside parties. During your exercise, consider exploring the following questions from the Microsoft publication "A Framework for Cybersecurity Information Sharing and Risk Reduction" (*https://www .microsoft.com/en-us/download/details.aspx?id=45516*) when confronting the topic of information sharing:

- Who should share information?
- What should be shared?
- When should it be shared?
- What is the quality and utility of what is shared?
- How should it be shared?
- Why is it being shared?
- What can be done with the information?

Organizations should consider well in advance the nuances of sharing information, such as maintaining confidentiality, while also balancing the interests of other internal stakeholders, particularly the legal team.

Gaps in the Incident Response Plan

One of the most crucial parts of effective incident response is the incident response plan. *Computer Security Incident Handling Guide* (NIST SP 800-61r2) provides excellent guidance on what should be included in this plan. One critical component is a *charter*, which defines what an incident is and includes the mission statement, goals and objectives, and authority of the team. The plan should also define the members of the incident response team, their roles and responsibilities, and the incident severity levels set by the organization. It should spell out an organized incident response approach and communication protocols.

In addition, the plan should designate a specific person to oversee testing (to avoid the diffusion of responsibility) and define a testing frequency; at a minimum, the plan should be tested once a year, and ideally twice a year. Testing the plan using an exercise allows the team to collaborate in an organized manner to resolve the incident, learn from one another, and potentially find gaps in the plan itself.

Even in the best-written incident response plan, tabletop exercises often uncover areas for improvement. Take time during the tabletop to document these gaps so the plan can be updated accordingly. You want to find the weaknesses during these exercises—not in the heat of a real incident.

The Efficacy of Processes and Procedures

Some organizations have predefined plans to respond to specific types of cybersecurity incidents. In addition to the incident response plan, you might want to validate the following:

- Playbooks that address a certain type of cybersecurity event or incident, such as ransomware; these playbooks provide in-depth guidance and thus require investments to keep up to date
- Incident escalation paths, which ensure that relevant members of technical and strategic teams are notified at the appropriate time via a predefined communications channel
- Incident identification and notification procedures, which help the organization identify an incident at all levels and notify relevant parties
- Containment procedures, which dictate how to execute containment efforts in tandem with business continuity plans
- External party notifications, such as required communications to government entities

A tabletop exercise doesn't necessarily need to validate all processes and procedures. Instead, it could home in on a single item of concern, such as a recently updated process or a change to the organization that has the potential to impact incident response efforts.

Compliance with Notification Requirements

Of particular salience, a tabletop provides a low-stress environment to evaluate the requirements related to notifying external parties. You've likely had the unpleasant experience of receiving a data breach notification letter from a financial institution, healthcare provider, or other business. That organization probably sent the letter to comply with a breach notification obligation.

Since the early 2000s, laws have imposed specific requirements for notifying consumers of the loss of protected data. In the United States, California pioneered data breach notification laws in 2002, and all 50 states now have their own variations. In the European Union, the GDPR legislation codifies, among other things, data breach notification rules. Other countries have followed suit, including Australia, China, and even Barbados (as noted earlier in the chapter).

However, each data breach law defines sensitive data sets differently and outlines its own notification process. Perhaps most importantly, some define slightly different temporal requirements and thresholds at which a notification is required. For example, one data breach law may require notification to an authority within 72 hours of a *suspected* compromise of a data set, while another may allow seven business days for a *confirmed* compromise.

These data breach laws can quickly become cumbersome in even a simple cybersecurity incident. Consider the fictitious Executive Travel Experience (ETE), a publicly traded travel agency whose client list represents citizens from almost every US state, most Canadian provinces, several European countries, and a few Middle Eastern and Southeast Asian countries. Say ETE's information security team believes the threat actors may have had access to client data as well as employee data, including health plan information. ETE's employee base is mostly located in Chicago but has strategic account managers throughout the world.

Addressing the legal component of this relatively common scenario can become a beast in itself. ETE's legal team needs to consider, at a minimum:

- The nuances of data breach laws relating to almost every US state, Canadian province, and other impacted countries

- Notification requirements for each customer whose data was stolen

- In cases when the data involved was owned by a vendor and ETE had contractual requirements to safeguard it, whether ETE must notify the vendor

- Because ETE's health plan information was likely accessed, whether ETE must notify the US Department of Health and Human Services, which administers the Health Insurance Portability and Accountability Act (HIPAA)

- Whether the incident meets materiality, thus requiring ETE—as a publicly traded US company—to file SEC Form 8-K to notify investors

In addition, for each of these questions, ETE must consider temporal requirements for performing the notification. As you can see, a cybersecurity incident could easily balloon into a myriad of downstream tasks. A tabletop exercise allows you to identify and explore these tasks in a low-stress setting.

Business contracts with other organizations might also outline notification requirements. For example, they may stipulate that you must issue a notification if a specific data set is lost. Finally, consider whether you have an ethical or moral responsibility to notify impacted individuals or organizations, even if the incident doesn't meet a legislative or contractual bar. While these ethical guidelines are less black-and-white than legal requirements, organizations should still assess them when determining whom to notify during a tabletop exercise.

Residual Risk After Corrective Actions

After most cybersecurity incidents, an organization will examine the factors that caused or contributed to the incident, such as a failure of technical controls, policies, or end user education. Once it identifies these factors, the organization may make changes or technology investments to reduce the risk of recurrence. At this stage, performing a tabletop exercise can enable stakeholders to run through a similar cybersecurity incident and discuss those corrective measures. This step functions as an additional check to identify residual risk as well as another opportunity to fully assess the downstream impact of any changes.

Summary

In this chapter, we've discussed many of the common reasons organizations choose to perform tabletop exercises. Tabletops have quantifiable benefits, such as monetary savings during a data breach, as well as more qualitative ones, such as improved relationships among response team members. Your organization may want to perform a tabletop exercise for reasons that aren't listed in this chapter, but what matters most is that you understand and align with its goals when starting your tabletop exercise journey.

Questions

As you begin planning an upcoming tabletop exercise, take the time to contemplate the following questions (some may have readily apparent answers, while others may require investigation):

1. In performing a tabletop exercise, are there specific conditions (such as contractual or regulatory requirements) you must meet?
2. What are the intended primary and ancillary benefits of performing a tabletop exercise in your organization?
3. What lessons would you like to learn by performing a tabletop exercise?
4. What people, process, or technology factors would you like the tabletop exercise to test?

2

PLANNING THE
TABLETOP EXERCISE

Before you can develop the tabletop exercise, you need to lay its foundation. This chapter will walk you through that process, outlining the factors you should consider in the preparation and planning stage. The advice in this chapter comes from hundreds of conversations with our clients, who frequently ask the same several questions that you'll need to answer prior to constructing the tabletop exercise.

These foundational questions include the following: Who from the executive level is providing support? What are the organization's goals and objectives? What is the exercise's tenor? Whom should you invite? What logistics are involved, and who will be handling them? Those responsible for developing the tabletop exercise, as well as executives wanting to understand their function in the process, tend to care about the answers to these planning questions. After all, the exercise will take place in front of their peers, leadership, and vendors, and in such a situation, nobody wants to be caught off guard.

Securing Executive Sponsor Support

Perhaps the most important step to prepare for a tabletop exercise is securing support from an executive sponsor. The sponsor's exact role and identity will vary depending on the type of exercise you're pursuing, the maturity of the organization, and the participants in the exercise, but sponsors are generally two or more rungs higher on an organizational chart than the highest-ranking participant.

Choosing an Appropriate Executive Sponsor

Consider how you might choose the executive sponsor in each of the following tabletop exercise scenarios:

- Testing whether the organization's IT help desk is able to recognize a cybersecurity event and escalate the issue to the proper points of contact
- Testing the organization's ability to perform internal and external communications during a large, public-facing incident

In the first scenario, the highest level of management participating in the tabletop exercise would likely be the IT help desk manager. In this case, it would be appropriate for an information security officer, a security director, or someone in a similar position to function as the executive sponsor.

The second scenario would likely involve representatives from departments like marketing, legal, public relations, information technology, and information security, in addition to other cross-functional positions. Due to the level of visibility, range of functions, and likelihood that the exercise will include a variety of senior management, it would make sense to select the chief information officer, the chief operations officer, or a similar executive as the sponsor.

The executive sponsor should understand the processes being tested but doesn't necessarily need an in-depth mastery of the topic. Their primary value comes from their awareness of the organization's cultural norms, their long-standing relationships with a variety of employees, and their influence among those they are sponsoring. As you'll see when we cover the expectations of the executive sponsor, the occasional email from them may be all you need to move your stalled tabletop exercise along or get participants to focus on the event.

It might also be beneficial to select an executive sponsor with an interest in the goals and objectives of the tabletop scenario. (We'll cover these topics in "Defining the Exercise's Goals and Objectives" on page 26.) For example, if an organization wishes to educate stakeholders about recent privacy legislation, you might choose a senior executive in the legal department. Alternatively, if the organization hopes to rehearse public-facing aspects of an incident, such as how to communicate with the public, you might want to request a chief communications officer as the executive sponsor.

Outlining the Executive Sponsor's Responsibilities

Once you've identified the executive sponsor, what should you expect of this role? The executive sponsor won't construct the PowerPoint deck, nor will they compose meeting agendas for the tabletop participants. However, their participation will trigger meaningful engagement throughout the tabletop exercise.

The Announcement

Any new project involving a variety of participants will require some formal announcement. The executive sponsor should be a part of this announcement to clarify that the exercise is important to the organization and that they will track its progress and participate. The announcement should make clear to all participants that the executive sponsor has put their organizational weight behind the initiative.

Planning Meetings

Even the simplest tabletop exercise requires planning. The executive sponsor doesn't have to attend every planning meeting; however, they should join at least one of them—ideally the first, which lays the foundation for future planning and reinforces their support. Additionally, should the executive sponsor have concerns about the direction of the tabletop exercise, they're able to express these as early as possible. By attending these meetings, they can better understand the status of the exercise, make sure the plan aligns with the organization's interests, and help remedy potential roadblocks. Perhaps most importantly, their attendance reinforces their continued commitment to the exercise.

Communication

Whenever the opportunity presents itself, the executive sponsor should reiterate the importance of the exercise. In some cases, they may need to sell the exercise to peers. It's not uncommon to face resistance from individuals across the organization, including those at the executive level, who believe the exercise isn't important to their role or team. You'd be surprised by how often a simple email from the sponsor can magically clear schedules and rearrange priorities.

Furthermore, the executive sponsor likely oversees regular meetings at the organization. By making a few comments at the start of a meeting about how pleased they are with the exercise planning and thanking the group for devoting time thus far, they can communicate its importance.

Legal Concerns

The tabletop exercise's materials and discussions may benefit from guidance from the organization's legal counsel, who can weigh in on any issues that emerge during planning. This is particularly true for organizations that operate in a highly regulated industry or engage in business with other entities. Some organizations may also choose to have the legal team direct the exercise. In such cases, the executive sponsor may be a member of the organization's legal team, or a legal representative may serve as a co-sponsor. In all cases, the executive sponsor should be aware of any potential legal issues.

Attendance

Perhaps the most important obligation of the executive sponsor is to attend the tabletop exercise. The sponsor's name on the calendar invite will encourage attendees to prioritize the meeting and participate actively, rather than passively listen with their head focused on their email inbox. If the sponsor's presence creates a sense of stuffiness, however, you should make an effort to ensure that all participants feel comfortable speaking up—for example, by having the sponsor issue a friendly statement reinforcing the value of participation.

Participation

Keep in mind that the executive sponsor's attendance and comments during the tabletop exercise may have a chilling effect on the discussion. For this reason, their participation will likely be minimal and limited to short comments where their input is necessary.

This isn't a universal rule, however, and their input may depend on the specifics of the tabletop as well as the organization's culture. Above all, their participation should be purposeful and align with the exercise's goals and objectives.

Defining the Exercise's Goals and Objectives

In the business world, *goals* are understood to be broad, long-term results that an organization would like to achieve. *Objectives*, or intermediary steps in the pursuit of goals, are short term and defined with greater granularity. For example, a college senior at a four-year university studying information technology might have the goal of securing a job with an information security team. Their objectives might be to finish their degree, earn the Security+ certification, and land an internship. The objectives are specific and feed into the overall goal.

You might conceive of a tabletop exercise as either a goal or an objective. Say an organization has a goal of all key staff members becoming familiar with the incident response plan. A tabletop exercise may be only one of several steps it takes to familiarize them with the plan, making the exercise an objective. On the other hand, the successful completion of a tabletop exercise could itself be the goal, in which case objectives might be educating the staff about the incident response plan, exploring a ransomware event's impact on operations, or testing the incident management process.

Most organizations view the tabletop exercise as an apex event in line with a goal and treat it as the culmination of a series of preparatory tasks. Following this approach, let's examine a few common objectives for an exercise.

NOTE *Your organization likely has more than one relevant objective; to realize maximum value, you should try to define several before developing your tabletop exercise.*

Rehearsing the Incident Response Plan

When organizations create an incident response program, they typically first develop an incident response plan and playbooks with a corresponding incident response team, and then rehearse the plan via a tabletop exercise. This process allows the organization not only to determine whether the incident response plan meets its needs but also to find any holes in it.

Alternatively, organizations that already have a plan in place may also want to rehearse their plan to build confidence in its process and procedures.

Understanding Organizational Incident Response Roles

A common objective of a tabletop exercise is to help participants understand how a cybersecurity incident can quickly career beyond the realm of information security and involve a variety of nontechnical employees. To demonstrate this, you could develop a scenario that pulls in a wide range of participants.

Be thoughtful about whom you include, however. Otherwise, the participants may find themselves wondering why they're there. Rarely does a cybersecurity incident require only a small team, and a properly developed scenario can help participants—whether they come from marketing, legal, or finance—better understand their role in the response.

Organizations might also want to conduct such a tabletop exercise whenever there's turnover within the organization, changes in the team structure, or acquisitions and divestitures that shrink or grow the team. Each of these situations may impact who is a part of the response to an incident, and a tabletop exercise can help participants reorient themselves.

Assessing Vendor Response

External vendors often play a role in the incident response effort, whether they're a managed security services provider (MSSP), an external legal counsel, a breach coach, or some other entity. Even vendors that have little to do with information security, such as an organization that prints and mails statements for a financial institution, can become involved in an incident. Tabletop exercises are an excellent way to assess how well the vendor and organization coordinate during an incident and identify any gaps in the response. At a minimum, the tabletop exercise provides an opportunity for the internal information security team to foster a collaborative working relationship with the external vendor.

Evaluating Communication Processes

Communication processes can quickly break down during an incident if the organization is not well prepared, and requirements from cyber insurance and regulatory bodies only add to their complexity. Tabletop exercises are an excellent way to ensure that the organization has well-defined communication processes, knows who will handle internal and external notifications, and can meet any notification deadlines.

Senior-Level vs. Operational-Level Exercises

Tabletop exercises are typically divided into two camps: senior level and operational level. *Senior-level exercises* generally focus on strategic concerns of the business, organizational authorities, and decision-makers. *Operational-level exercises* address the technical, hands-on aspects of the response.

For example, if an objective of the exercise is to familiarize the communications department with the nuances of responding to a cybersecurity incident that has bubbled into the public domain, this would be a senior-level tabletop. Alternatively, if the focus is on the practicalities of implementing network containment strategies to mitigate the effects of malware, the exercise would be an operational-level tabletop.

Senior-level exercises typically bring together managerial roles from different departments, while technical-level exercises involve technical team members and some members of their management. Of course, technical employees can still use the exercise to discuss nontechnical issues, such as policy constraints, that pertain to their positions. Table 2-1 lists some topics appropriate for each type of exercise.

Table 2-1: Senior-Level vs. Operational-Level Exercise Topics

Incident scenario	Senior-level tabletop exercise	Operational-level tabletop exercise
Ransomware	Discuss the factors that determine whether to pay a ransom.	Walk through the restoration of critical systems after a ransomware attack.
Email compromise	Explore legal and regulatory concerns related to an uncontrolled release of personally identifiable information.	Assess backup communication systems in case primary systems (such as email) become compromised.

Incident scenario	Senior-level tabletop exercise	Operational-level tabletop exercise
Data breach	Respond to a media inquiry regarding a publicly known breach.	Rehearse the collection of key logs for investigatory purposes.
Third-party security incident	Explore the legal concerns involved in responding to a cybersecurity incident at a key third-party vendor.	Determine technical steps to sever network connectivity with a third-party vendor as a containment measure.
Distributed denial-of-service attack	Respond to losing the ability to deliver products and meet contractual deadlines.	Discuss technical steps to mitigate a denial-of-service attack.
Industrial control system compromise	Consider the impact of a network compromise for a system affecting product safety.	Discuss the feasibility of swiftly implementing containment methods in an operational technology environment.

The choice of a senior-level tabletop exercise doesn't necessarily mean that the organization is more mature. Instead, it reflects the focus of the tabletop. If the exercise explores strategic business issues, it's likely to be senior level. An organization doesn't need to have performed several operational-level tabletop exercises to "graduate" to senior-level exercises.

If an organization has the necessary resources, it might run connected operational-level and senior-level tabletops. These *tandem exercises* enable an organization to explore a single topic (such as ransomware) by focusing one session on the technical issues, then moving into a second session focused on strategic elements. Each session should be treated as its own self-contained tabletop exercise, with separate attendees and specific areas of focus. While tandem exercises are more resource intensive, they have several benefits:

- They take advantage of economies of scale during the planning process.
- They convey an incident's technical and strategic considerations.
- They engage roles across the business, demonstrating that a single cybersecurity event has wide-reaching implications.

With the proper planning, a tandem exercise also affords an opportunity to create a more dynamic experience. For example, a member of the operational-level tabletop cohort can give the senior-level tabletop cohort a briefing on technical issues the previous exercise attendees have observed and any actions they've taken. Chapters 6 and 7 cover example scenarios you could use in tandem exercises.

Determining Who Should Participate

In addition to whether you're performing a senior- or operational-level tabletop exercise, the scenario topic is what usually determines who should attend the tabletop. For example, if a senior-level tabletop exercise explored data breach obligations, members of the legal team would be at the top of the attendance list, and if an operational-level tabletop exercise focused on technical controls and strategies to contain a ransomware outbreak, participants should include information technology and information security staff.

Other times, the incident response plan will define the list of participants for you. This plan should contain roles, usually broken into operational and senior level, to call upon during an incident, such as human resources, disaster recovery, and system administrators. The incident response plan should also define a primary and secondary point of contact for each role, both of whom you could invite to the exercise.

In some cases, the exercise's topic might be appropriate for a mix of senior- and lower-level staff members; however, combining these parties may be unwise. In mixed groups, the conversation could focus on issues that are of interest to one group but not the other, causing a subset of the participants to check out. Furthermore, the presence of participants from the upper echelon of the organization may have a chilling effect, discouraging lower-level staff members from contributing valuable feedback.

Finally, be selective about who should join. Casting too wide of a net will leave participants without significant opportunities for participation, and they may end up frustrated that they wasted their time. The best tabletops tend to have 10 to 15 attendees, making them large enough to include many roles but small enough to create a collaborative environment. However, don't be afraid to run a tabletop exercise with fewer attendees. Even small information technology and information security teams of only two to four staff members may find it valuable to discuss the response to a cybersecurity incident.

External Vendors

Your organization likely works with a variety of vendors that impact its information security posture. You may want to include them in your exercise if they'll have a role to play during a cybersecurity incident. For example, consider the following vendors:

- An outsourced, part-time virtual chief information security officer (vCISO)
- An MSSP security operations center (SOC) that is responsible for identifying, containing, and addressing cybersecurity incidents
- A printing and mailing firm that sends monthly mortgage statements, account summaries, and other printed material for a financial institution
- The communications and marketing firm responsible for maintaining social media channels and updating the organization's website
- A manufacturer that remotely logs in to a specialized metal fabrication system to perform troubleshooting and firmware updates
- An offsite storage facility responsible for securing tape backups

- Physical security resources tasked with providing access to buildings and securing facilities
- A vendor that operates a Software as a Service (SaaS) application to provide weather forecast data for flight planning services

A tabletop exercise is a way for the organization to pull vendors into the response process to learn how they could offer support as well as any limitations they have.

Perhaps most importantly, if a cybersecurity incident involved a failure originating from a vendor, such as a vendor-maintained system with poor password practices, understanding how the vendor would escalate the incident to the organization would enable both parties to identify potential gaps in the relationship. This last point is especially salient, as the internet is rife with stories about such failures. Consider bullets three and five from the preceding list: a printing and mailing firm and a metal manufacturer don't serve an information security role, but a failure in either could cause a major incident nonetheless.

However, avoid pulling too many vendors into a tabletop exercise. In some cases, it may not be appropriate to invite more than a single vendor. Each vendor has a unique relationship with the organization and is under pressure to perform satisfactorily; if they don't, they know their contract might not be renewed. You should always take great care to reinforce that the exercise is an opportunity to forge a stronger relationship and isn't intended to put the vendor in the hot seat.

Finally, if you plan to discuss sensitive topics, it may be inappropriate for an external party to join. Their inclusion should be purposeful and directly align with your goals and objectives. Don't extend such invitations unless the executive sponsor and internal legal counsel have given their permission, and follow the organization's existing information-sharing procedures.

CASE STUDY: A VENDOR-FOCUSED EXERCISE

High Five Commercial (HFC), which owned marquee commercial properties in the southeastern United States, wanted to perform a tabletop exercise to gauge its preparation for its number one risk: an information system failure related to its building technologies, which consisted of banks of elevators, HVAC systems, and controlled entry systems used to grant physical access. HFC invited its elevator maintenance provider, Mitchell Elevators, to participate, as the provider had recently begun diagnosing issues by remotely connecting to the computers running the elevators. Given that many of HFC's buildings were 20 stories or more, issues impacting elevators could plausibly present a major safety hazard, not to mention an accessibility problem for many tenants.

The tabletop exercise scenario was simple: malware had infected the elevator computer systems while Mitchell Elevators performed maintenance using

(continued)

a USB device containing malicious software. Although Mitchell Elevators wasn't pleased with the premise, it conceded that there was precedent for it, as such attacks had occurred in the industry in very rare circumstances. Regardless, the Mitchell Elevators crew remained good sports; HFC was a client they could not afford to lose.

In the discussion of the scenario, which involved the elevator systems failing around the holidays, several findings emerged:

- Mitchell Elevators believed the event would likely require replacing several computer systems at the HFC properties, and because of logistical factors (namely, the elevators were made by a German engineering firm, and spare parts were not readily available), the replacement would take several days.

- Because the incident occurred over the holidays, Mitchell Elevators wasn't sure they had enough technicians available to perform such a labor-intensive replacement.

- The passwords Mitchell Elevators used to connect to a virtual private network to remotely access the elevator computers did not conform to HFC's password policy. However, HFC had not informed Mitchell Elevators of this policy.

The tabletop wasn't adversarial; prior to the exercise, HFC emphasized that it didn't intend to find fault with Mitchell Elevators, and when gaps emerged, its staff didn't criticize the vendor. The outcome? Mitchell Elevators adjusted its password practices on all HFC systems to conform to HFC's policy. HFC requested that Mitchell Elevators maintain replacement backup computer systems to eliminate the need to import them on-demand from Germany and ensure that there was staff available to assist with large issues at an HFC property during the holidays. Mitchell Elevators was happy to oblige and built the costs into the next contract year. Perhaps most importantly, HFC's and Mitchell Elevators' staff bolstered their trust in each other.

Legal Support

It isn't uncommon for some form of litigation to emerge after a cybersecurity incident, so it's essential to include legal resources in the incident response process. Additionally, because the initial hours of an incident may become a focal point in future litigation, an organization's legal resources must provide guidance about maintaining *legal privilege*, a rule that can keep communications and other work products confidential. Misconceptions regarding privilege run rampant, so organizations should rely on qualified legal guidance on this front.

For organizations that have in-house counsel, the process of including legal team members in the tabletop exercise may be as simple as sending a friendly email. Organizations without in-house legal counsel should pull in an external legal resource to participate in the tabletop exercise. External counsel usually bills hourly, but because the legal team may appreciate this opportunity to strengthen the bond with its client, it may categorize the exercise as relationship building and participate free of charge.

In some cases, the organization may discover potential legal issues that fall outside the scope of its external legal counsel. For example, the organization might need legal guidance on performing data breach notifications in another country, while the retained external counsel focuses solely on employment issues and trade secrets. In such a situation, the organization may decide to secure specialized supplemental external counsel to fill this gap and support its unique needs.

The Development Team

You also need to consider who will participate in the tabletop exercise development process. It is perfectly acceptable for one person to create all facets of a tabletop exercise; however, the most effective exercises include multiple individuals with different skills, personalities, and job tenure.

To diversify the team, consider including members from outside the cybersecurity field. Employees from human resources could be helpful if, for instance, incident responders neglected to contact HR during a past incident to protect an employee from disciplinary actions. Audit and risk management, which have a vested interest in identifying and remediating risk within the organization, could be included as well. You might also find it beneficial to include a senior employee who can open doors and understand the nuances of relationships between departments.

Most optimal development teams are composed of two or three individuals. This lets the team divide the workload, share their knowledge, and add creativity to the exercise. It also provides redundancy in case one team member becomes ill before the exercise, is reassigned to an emergency project, or leaves the organization. We'll go over some common roles for team members here, but keep in mind that some exercises might not need every role. Don't include roles unless they provide clear value.

The Development Lead

The development lead is responsible for planning and executing the tabletop exercise. In organizations that maintain a mature incident response plan, the plan usually defines the individual tasked with this role. Ideally, the plan should identify a *specific* individual and not a generic category, such as information security, which could diffuse responsibility. If the plan doesn't specify an individual, choose a more senior employee based in information technology, information security, or similar. The development lead should have the following:

- An in-depth knowledge of how the organization functions
- An understanding of the information systems and security controls in place
- A leadership role, likely responsible for incident response
- The respect of many employees across the organization

- Excellent interpersonal communication skills and a proven track record of building coalitions across functions
- Natural and relaxed presentation skills
- Existing relationships outside of information technology

If no candidate possesses all these traits, prioritize the soft skills. You can always make up for a lack of technical knowledge with other members of the team; however, to create a successful exercise, you'll need a leader with superb communication skills and the ability to galvanize others.

While the development lead should be a senior employee, this person should be a few rungs down the organizational ladder from the executive sponsor.

The Facilitator

The facilitator is the face of the tabletop exercise during the event. The development lead is a logical choice for this role, as they are intimately familiar with the scenario and various ways of exploring it; however, it is perfectly acceptable to have separate individuals fulfill each role. In addition, the facilitator should be:

- At ease presenting in front of audiences composed of their peers and senior leadership
- Skilled at keeping the discussion on track while simultaneously identifying additional points that warrant attention
- Able to tactfully and respectfully encourage participants to engage in the tabletop exercise and avoid one or two participants dominating the event
- Adept at quickly building a rapport with attendees to encourage a wider participation
- Able to think on their feet
- Comfortable with the specific intended attendees (such as executives)

Even if all other facets of the development process execute flawlessly, the facilitator could make or break the tabletop exercise. Chapter 4 discusses the facilitation role in depth.

The Subject Matter Expert

Depending on the exercise topic, it may be beneficial to pull in a subject matter expert who can weigh in on issues pertaining to specific systems that are less familiar to other development team members. For example, if the scenario focuses on the organization's new cloud environment, a cloud infrastructure expert could ensure that the team understands the technical nuances of the topic. Other scenarios that could benefit from a subject matter expert include the following:

- An energy company whose pipelines contain unique operational technology systems wants to explore how threat actors might alter its pipeline safety systems.

- A credit union wants to explore how threat actors could compromise the global financial payment system SWIFT.

- A cruise ship operator plans to explore how a compromise of a ship-wide wireless internet system could impact guest safety or ship operations.

In each of these situations, the development team would need in-depth knowledge of information systems to craft a relevant and believable tabletop exercise. Note, though, that a subject matter expert doesn't necessarily need to focus on technical aspects of the exercise. The expert may come from legal, marketing, or other teams.

Finally, it may be appropriate to also have the subject matter expert attend the tabletop itself as a passive member in the audience. If a participant asks an in-depth question about a specific system that the facilitator isn't able to address, the subject matter expert can provide immediate clarification.

The Trusted Agent

If you plan to use a consultant to develop the tabletop exercise, or you aren't personally familiar with the topic and its participants, consider appointing an internal trusted agent. The trusted agent is essentially a type of subject matter expert assigned to work with an external consultant. (For more on working with outside consultants, see "Outsourcing Tabletop Exercises" on page 47.) The trusted agent should know the details of the scenario and can suggest alterations to the consultant based on their knowledge of the organization.

Trusted agents are useful in large enterprises consisting of tens of thousands of employees, where the development team may not personally know the participants or clearly understand the workings of the relevant teams. However, as someone who will have inside knowledge of the exercise scenario, the trusted agent generally shouldn't participate in the tabletop itself. If they must participate, they should make minimal contributions and avoid revealing details of the scenario not yet known to the participants.

The Observer

Some organizations may wish to have a passive observer participate in the exercise. The passive observer does as the name suggests: they observe the tabletop without interacting. Reasons to use an observer include the following:

- Enabling an interested party to understand the processes involved in responding to a cybersecurity incident

- Allowing a representative from legal to better understand unexpected legal issues that may emerge during an incident

Take care to ensure that the observer won't impact the tabletop exercise. For example, the presence of a chief executive at a tabletop about the help desk could stifle constructive communication.

The Evaluator

Given the number of tasks the facilitator must handle, they might find it helpful to enlist someone else to evaluate the process and note any weakness or strengths discovered during the exercise. Like the observer, the evaluator is a passive role. The evaluator could even be the observer or a co-facilitator, a position discussed further in Chapter 5.

Logistical Considerations

Before the exercise itself, you'll have to perform many of the event planning activities necessary for any large activity. For example, in-person tabletop exercises will require conference rooms with the appropriate amenities. You must also identify and address any attendee concerns. No one should enter the tabletop without the opportunity to ask questions, correct any misperceptions, and douse their residual fears.

This section will also cover various time-consuming tasks that could be added to the development team's list of to-dos. Depending on factors like the size of the development team, the style of the tabletop exercise, and the number of attendees, you might wish to assign a project manager to some of these tasks.

Hosting Remote vs. In-Person Exercises

During the COVID-19 pandemic, many organizations began performing tabletop exercises remotely. While tabletops can succeed in a remote environment, in-person exercises tend to be more intimate. The facilitator and team members can greet participants personally as they enter the physical space and engage in small talk. During the actual tabletop exercise, the facilitator can also read body language and assess participants' behaviors, which can help clarify their reactions to points brought up in the exercise. Remote exercises immediately handicap the facilitator; the usual handshake won't occur, and visual cues may be easier to miss or absent altogether. In addition, in-person exercises make it easier for participants to interact directly with each other to explore certain issues, perhaps during a lunch break.

Some organizations opt for hybrid tabletop exercises, with some participants physically present in a conference room and others connected via video or phone. Facilitating a hybrid tabletop exercise is especially challenging, however, because the in-person participants will inevitably command the forum, and both they and the facilitator can easily forget about the remote attendees. Chapter 4 explores other factors you should consider when facilitating such an exercise.

When deciding whether to hold a remote or in-person tabletop exercise, ask yourself why the exercise is being performed. Often, one of its objectives is to form stronger bonds among participants, which often happens due to the inevitable "watercooler moments" that occur before and after the exercise. If the goal is to bring together employees who are largely unfamiliar with each other, in-person tabletop exercises will pay the most dividends and are worth the investment. However, if participants are already very familiar with each other, a remote tabletop exercise may be sufficient.

Also consider the organizational culture. Some companies don't use remote work due to their centralized work locations, industry norms, or other factors. Senior-level staff members also have a tendency to favor in-person collaboration and are generally assigned to a central location like the company's headquarters, so remote tabletop exercises might not make sense for this group.

Determining the Duration

While there are always exceptions, most effective tabletop exercises clock in at two to three hours. More time devoted to the exercise does not necessarily mean that it will be more comprehensive; eventually, you'll reach a point of diminishing returns as the discussion and attention spans start to wane. That said, consider these additional factors when planning the exercise's duration:

- Senior-level tabletop exercises are more likely to encounter time constraints, and it is rare for executives to participate in a tabletop exercise longer than two hours.

- For remote exercises, shorter tabletops are more prudent. In today's distraction-rich environment, it's all too easy to dive back into email or chat conversations when not in view of your peers.

It is important to get the duration right; if participants feel that their time wasn't effectively used, they'll be less willing to participate in future exercises.

Choosing a Date and Time

Before planning any of the logistics, identify calendar constraints. For senior-level tabletop exercises, timing could be the most critical factor to consider when you are planning the event. The senior leadership of some organizations may meet only once a quarter. In these cases, you may have to first define the target date and then work backward.

Let's examine a few other considerations for choosing a date:

- Avoid Mondays and Fridays. It's very common for employees to take one of these days off to extend their weekend.

- Factor in cultural norms that can influence vacation schedules, such as long summer breaks in certain countries, holidays unique to certain faiths or ethnicities, and the start of hunting or fishing season.

- Add in buffers around significant holidays to account for longer vacations.

- Be considerate of attendees with school-age children and account for the academic calendar.

- Avoid the dates of major operating system patches, such as Microsoft's monthly Patch Tuesday, especially for operational-level tabletop exercises in which technical employees will participate.

- Avoid times of year that are busy or dedicated to high-profile work. These could include the holiday shopping season for a retailer, the end of a semester for a university, or days when publicly traded companies announce their earnings reports.

- For international teams, be cognizant of various holidays specific to particular countries or a workweek that deviates from the usual Monday through Friday.

Don't be surprised if a conflict emerges after you've chosen an initial date for the exercise. Unless you have a hard deadline, it's acceptable to reschedule the tabletop exercise. Keep an alternative date in mind from the beginning, but don't disclose it until it's needed; in most organizations, competing priorities always emerge, and the event with the most flexibility (such as the one with a known alternative date) will likely be the one that gets rescheduled.

Choosing the specific time of day for the exercise also requires considering a variety of factors. For example, some organizations may have a culture of avoiding early or late meetings. Others have significant obligations at certain times; for example, a distribution company may need to process overnight orders in the morning. Finally, for global organizations with employees spread between, say, the United Kingdom and Canada, you'll need to aim for a later start for the United Kingdom employees and an early start for their Canadian counterparts.

A common strategy is to hold the tabletop exercise during lunch. An exercise that takes place between 11 AM and 2 PM provides an opportunity to cater lunch and break for a meal. (Be sure to ask about attendees' dietary requirements ahead of time and accommodate any requests.) During the lunch break, attendees and the facilitator can mingle, discussing issues that have emerged in the scenario thus far and identifying future collaboration opportunities.

Securing a Facility

Unless the tabletop exercise will be held remotely, the development team must find a facility. Typically, you'll reserve a conference room available to the organization or rent a space at an alternative location.

Conference Rooms

Many organizations have multiple conference rooms to choose from, and planning a tabletop exercise well in advance lets you select an appropriate one. What makes for the "right" conference room? Consider the following factors:

Convenience for attendees Some organizations have sprawling campuses or multiple buildings scattered across an urban center. Take stock of the attendee list and make a good-faith effort to choose a location that is central to the majority of attendees.

Priority of stakeholders　While you should try to choose a location that is convenient for all attendees, you may need to make concessions for a single person or a small group that is central to the tabletop exercise. For example, if it is critical to have the CISO as a part of the tabletop exercise but they can only attend at a particular facility with a conference room, that need may outweigh the convenience of other attendees.

Audiovisual needs　If the tabletop has specific audiovisual needs— for example, projectors, cameras, microphones, screens, and other accessories that enable a participant to join remotely or help convey the material effectively—select the conference room that is most likely to accommodate them. Chapter 4 explores this topic in more depth.

Number of attendees　You should know the number of attendees well in advance to select an appropriately sized conference room. A room that's too small will be uncomfortable for attendees, while one that's too large can feel cavernous and unwelcoming.

Social distancing　While we all hope we don't face another global pandemic anytime soon, COVID-19 taught us that there are times when you need to accommodate some degree of social distancing. (Of course, if any participant is feeling unwell or showing symptoms of illness, it's best to stay home.)

Accessibility　Some employees may have accessibility requirements, such as wheelchair access or assistive technologies for those with hearing or visual impairments.

Facilitator space　The conference room should have adequate space for the facilitator to set up and present in front of attendees.

Also consider the optics of the conference room you choose. Hosting a tabletop exercise in the musty old conference room in the basement conveys the message that the exercise isn't a priority, and negative first impressions can be hard to overcome.

External Sites

Not every organization will have access to the appropriate facilities. In these cases, you can rent an alternative facility, such as a hotel, co-working space, or banquet room at a restaurant or brewery. When evaluating potential off-site facilities, consider the following questions:

- Is the facility conveniently located for most attendees? Choosing a location requiring a two-hour commute is a surefire way to alienate attendees before the event starts.

- Does the facility meet the development team's technology requirements? These requirements usually include a projector, a screen, Wi-Fi, and easily accessible electrical outlets.

- Can the facility support remote attendees? If a handful of attendees are connecting remotely, select a higher-quality facility with embedded cameras and audio devices to better enable their participation. You'll also need sufficient internet bandwidth.

- Is the facility private? Renting a space with significant foot traffic (such as a hotel conference room near the lobby reception area) may attract unwanted attention from curious passersby.

- Does the facility have amenities to make the tabletop exercise more enjoyable? These may include beverage or meal service and comfortable seating.

Choosing an external site can mitigate any potential downsides of using organizational facilities. Meeting in the executive conference room on the highest floor of the corporate headquarters may intimidate certain attendees, making them less likely to speak up. At an external site, participants might be more likely to offer constructive criticism of the organization. Plus, the external location could present an opportunity for a post-tabletop bonding experience, such as a meal or activity.

However, always evaluate the appropriateness of using the outside space. Attendees may find themselves discussing sensitive topics, such as the organization's weaknesses, so the space should be private, and if the organization works with unique trade secrets or classified weapons systems, working off-site might not be an option.

Setting the Tone

Before the tabletop exercise, determine the tone of your interactions with your participants. While there is no one-size-fits-all formula, consider the following approaches:

Educational   If the participants are new to tabletops or to cybersecurity, or if the purpose of the tabletop is to validate your processes after a process change, you may want to take a more educational and hand-holding approach. Place emphasis on aligning suggested actions to the incident response plan, as well as educating participants about their roles.

Collaborative   If the participants have a range of experience in cybersecurity, have likely experienced a cybersecurity incident in the recent past, and want to explore how well any documented processes will hold up in a cybersecurity incident, take a more collaborative approach. This could include helping participants explore issues as they emerge while also raising additional areas of concern that haven't been addressed.

Challenging   In the most advanced kind of exercise, participants are likely industry veterans who have experienced many cybersecurity issues, and the organization's processes are well documented. For such an audience, you can afford to take a more tactfully aggressive stance by challenging participants' answers, pointing out areas of weakness, and pushing the team to improve.

In general, consider the industry and organizational experience of those in the tabletop exercise and let that dictate the tone. Industry veterans probably don't want to face a drill sergeant, but they might benefit from a facilitator who is able to tactfully explore questionable or problematic answers and bring deficiencies to light.

Also consider the organization's cybersecurity maturity spectrum. If the company has historically treated cybersecurity as an afterthought, a collaborative or hand-holding approach would be beneficial, as it would meet participants where they are. The team could get their feet wet, discussing and learning basic response steps and best practices, instead of making their first foray into incident response during an actual engagement.

Lastly, if the organization is primarily performing the tabletop to gather stakeholders and build trust, the tone of the tabletop should reflect this goal. But if the organization wishes to dig into the roles and responsibilities expected of stakeholders, it may be prudent to adopt a more aggressive demeanor. However, always remain professional, polite, and tactful. Adopting a challenging approach doesn't give you a license to be condescending, insulting, or overly pedantic.

Make sure the development team (including the executive sponsor) agrees upon the tone from the outset of the exercise's development and remain consistent through the entire process, including in email communications and summaries.

Notifying and Preparing Exercise Attendees

Once you've selected a date and time and secured a facility, it's time to begin communicating with your expected attendees and other interested parties. In short, you must formally announce the tabletop exercise. This notification shouldn't be haphazard but rather part of a multipronged effort to clarify the exercise's goals and objectives, as well as what you expect from attendees. Some participants might respond with a battery of questions, and an effective communication strategy can allay any fears far in advance of the exercise. This section describes several components of the strategy used to prepare attendees for the exercise.

The Executive Checkpoint

One way to initially announce the basic details of a tabletop exercise is via the executive sponsor. It's likely that your sponsor regularly communicates with a larger team about business updates, the status of initiatives, hiring, and so on. These checkpoints provide an opportunity for the sponsor to discuss the exercise, explain its purpose, and describe why the organization has chosen to invest in the activity. Because the sponsor is in a position of authority, they can also communicate the importance of the exercise.

In their message, it could be helpful for the executive sponsor to highlight a recent cybersecurity incident familiar to the workforce, whether it be a high-profile news story or an issue that occurred within the organization itself. Ideally, this should help participants understand why the tabletop is being performed. In addition, the executive sponsor can briefly name the members of the development team, the development lead, and the facilitator, as well as disclose next steps.

Most importantly, this message shouldn't go into much depth and should convey a positive attitude. If the sponsor strikes a negative tone (for example, "I know no one wants to do this, but let's just get through it"), attendees might get the impression that this is just another check-the-box affair not worth their effort.

The Initial Email Notification

Following the executive sponsor's comments, it's time to connect with the attendees. For the sake of consistency, assign a single person to perform all communications going forward. This may be the project manager, the facilitator, the development lead, or another designated member of the development team. For some larger organizations, appointing a member of a communications team can ensure alignment with communication norms.

The communication lead should ideally email the attendees during the same week as the executive sponsor's announcement. Quickly emailing attendees can prevent any concerns from metastasizing. This email should succinctly convey key facts. Though it shouldn't attempt to answer every possible question from participants, it should direct them to someone who can address any concerns.

The following is a sample email constructed for an organization that has never performed a tabletop exercise or whose attendees may have many questions:

> Happy Friday!
>
> During the quarterly all-hands meeting, Jamie Winter announced an initiative that our company has been working on for the past several weeks. Next month, we will be performing our very first cybersecurity tabletop exercise.
>
> Our Executive Team has requested that a tabletop exercise be performed due to our recent alignment with the Payment Card Industry standards. Plus, this exercise will help gauge the company's readiness for a cybersecurity incident, identify any gaps in our response, and provide an opportunity for us to collaborate across teams while responding to a simulated incident.
>
> Our tabletop exercise will be taking place on April 3 between 10:30 AM and 1:30 PM. It will occur at our 318 Smith St. location, in the Evergreen Conference Room. Lunch will be provided.
>
> If you're receiving this email, it means that your participation is requested in the tabletop exercise. If you are unable to attend due to preexisting obligations, please plan on having a delegate attend in your place. No preparation or prereading is required.

The tabletop will not be a test of any one individual's or team's ability to respond. This is an opportunity to collaborate and improve.

The tabletop exercise Development Team (myself, Michael Murray, Diana Spinelli, and Jay Bell) recognizes that this may be a new experience for some. We're available to answer any questions you may have and will also set up an optional discussion session on March 20 at 10 AM and again on March 22 at 4 PM in the Evergreen Conference Room. Any questions are welcome. Of course, should any questions pop up before these sessions, you're welcome to respond to this email or stop by my office.

Thank you in advance for your support of this initiative.

Alphonse Moffit
Tabletop Exercise Development Lead

This email is friendly, references support from the executive sponsor (Jamie Winter), provides assurance that the tabletop exercise is not an intensive event, and offers opportunities for participants to pose questions either in a group setting or directly to the development lead.

Calendar Invitations

Immediately after sending the notification email, the communications lead should send calendar invitations to each invitee. This calendar invitation should, at a minimum, contain:

- The text from the initial email notification
- Logistical information, such as the timing and location
- Language helping the recipient distinguish between any discussion sessions and the actual tabletop exercise

Sending calendar invitations also provides an initial opportunity to identify any scheduling conflicts. If an attendee declines an invitation, the development team can make adjustments. Determine whether all parties have actually accepted the calendar invitations, and if they haven't, reach out via phone or email.

Also block out time on the calendars of any stakeholders for a debrief immediately following the tabletop exercise. If several key participants have to run to their next meeting right after a two-hour tabletop exercise, the evaluation phase will be impaired. We discuss the evaluation phase in Chapter 5.

The Discussion Session

The optional discussion session is an opportunity for attendees to ask questions before the tabletop exercise occurs. You can treat these sessions like a professor's office hours; attendees or other interested stakeholders can casually raise lingering concerns. The development lead and possibly additional members from the development team should plan on joining, and you should try to offer at least two sessions to account for conflicts.

In addition to helping ease attendee concerns, discussion sessions allow the exercise facilitator to bond with attendees prior to the tabletop exercise. Simply shaking hands, chatting about activities for the upcoming weekend, or knowing that a particular attendee is a new aunt provides valuable conversation fodder for the day of the tabletop exercise.

Finally, these discussions can surface common themes that the development team or executive sponsor might need to address. For example, if several attendees tell you, "We heard this exercise will be used to justify outsourcing more of the information security team," you can quickly address that concern before the exercise begins.

Informal Touchpoints

In addition to structured interactions such as the discussion sessions, the development team and executive sponsor can try to create informal touchpoints with attendees. Think of these as watercooler moments, those impromptu gatherings where employees discuss topics ranging from sports to the latest office news. If the opportunity arises, the development team members and executive sponsor can casually ask individual attendees how they feel about the upcoming exercise. It's during these informal interactions that employees may be most likely to reveal underlying concerns.

For example, an informal touchpoint with a tabletop participant in the office breakroom could reveal that they are worried about the exercise's time commitment or fear looking foolish as a new employee. While these comments may seem trivial, investing the time to allay these concerns will yield a better tabletop exercise.

Finally, it's important that the members of the development team and the executive sponsor continually share these concerns with each other. If all members of the development team hear the same concern from different sources, it's an indication that they need to provide additional clarification on a certain topic.

The Final Reminder

Approximately three business days before the event, send a reminder to all tabletop attendees. This reminder gives you one last chance to change the scenario if someone in an important role is unable to attend. For example, if your scenario focuses on the legal obligations of an organization that loses employee data and the legal representative has a family emergency, you may need to quickly alter the scenario or reschedule the exercise altogether.

Alternatively, you could use the absence of a key participant as an opportunity to provide nuance to the scenario. Decision-makers will be forced to adjust on the fly to the participant's absence—a circumstance that could certainly arise during a real-world event. This option is appropriate for tabletop exercises that aim to stress-test existing processes or discover single sources of failure, a common issue in responding to cybersecurity incidents. If the remaining participants all defer to the missing representative from legal, the development team has just discovered their first (and very important) recommendation.

Scenario Confidentiality

While it's fine for members of the organization to know that a tabletop exercise is on the horizon, it's important to maintain a degree of confidentiality about the scenario, goals, and objectives. Some participants may be nervous and ask to know about the scenario ahead of time. However, the confidentiality of the scenario is critical to the success of the tabletop exercise for several reasons.

First, during an actual incident, parties involved in the response will be immersed in the "fog of war"; they won't immediately be sure of the incident's impact on the organization, how the organization was attacked, and other factors. Tabletop exercises should be no different. Not releasing details prior to the exercise will leave participants surprised by the scenario as it unfolds and require them to make quick decisions, as they would during an incident.

Secondly, if participants know the details of the exercise, they tend to arrive with scripted replies to demonstrate they know the correct answer. One of the many reasons to perform a tabletop exercise is to have participants discuss the pros and cons of potential responses, recognize shortcomings in technology or organizational processes, and bring forward their particular interests. These discussions occur as participants collaborate, a process that is impaired when they're allowed to know details ahead of time.

When a senior-level invitee requests access to the tabletop exercise materials, it may not be easy to tell them, "No, sorry, you're not entitled to this material." But all is not lost—there are a few strategies to head off these requests:

- Prior to the exercise, warn the executive sponsor that participants may ask to view the materials and have the executive sponsor agree that the materials shouldn't be released in advance.

- Consider developing a "rules of engagement" document agreed to by the executive sponsor and development team stating that the scenario won't be provided in advance. Refer anyone requesting the materials to these rules of engagement.

- Ask the executive sponsor to speak with the person making the request and advocate for keeping the tabletop exercise confidential. Often, the conversation may reveal other concerns (such as the risk of being embarrassed in front of peers).

- When you start planning the exercise, meet with the stakeholders most likely to request the materials and discuss the rationale for not providing them in advance. Reinforce that the purpose of the tabletop exercise isn't to find fault in any one individual but to collaborate.

- Provide a few high-level details regarding the scenario that won't compromise the entire narrative.
- Reinforce that the intention of the tabletop is not to publicly flog a participant for not taking the proper steps.

In some cases, your attempts to keep the scenario confidential will fail. If a determined chief executive officer, majority owner, or board member requests access to the materials, they can barrel over your executive sponsor. On the bright side, having an executive take an interest in the tabletop exercise is an opportunity to demonstrate that there isn't anything to fear about it, and in the next event, you can make a special effort to get this person to buy into keeping the scenario confidential now that a relationship has been built.

Opposition from Invitees

Some individuals might oppose the tabletop exercise, either actively (such as by criticizing the format, questioning its value, or offering other less-than-positive feedback) or passively (by avoiding meetings, not RSVPing, or simply not prioritizing the event, for example).

Some of the common reasons for opposition include:

- Fear that the tabletop exercise will reveal a particular team's shortcomings
- A concern that a tabletop exercise or its findings will significantly impact their workload
- A preexisting interpersonal conflict that makes it uncomfortable for participants to work together

Regardless of the reasons for the opposition, the development team must identify early signs of it, such as individuals doing the following:

- Openly citing reasons to not perform the tabletop exercise, such as "Now isn't the time for a tabletop exercise when we have 20 other projects that are more important"
- Indicating displeasure nonverbally, such as crossing their arms or rolling their eyes
- Not engaging with basic requests, such as RSVPing to events or responding to email

Addressing opposition is the development team's responsibility, but how they go about it depends on the situation. One or more of the following methods will generally suffice:

- Ask the opposing party about their concerns and take the time to listen. Acknowledge and validate their feelings.
- If possible, offer to weave their concerns into the tabletop exercise. For example, if an individual is concerned that the organization's disaster recovery procedures are inadequate and the time allotted to the

exercise would be better spent discussing this issue, add this issue to the tabletop exercise focusing on this topic.

- Acknowledge that the upcoming tabletop exercise may not confront the opposing party's concerns, but offer to include the issue in future exercise scenarios.
- If the participant fears that the exercise may expose professional shortcomings and place their job in jeopardy, reassure them that the purpose isn't to find fault and assign blame.

Often, these conversations can occur over a cup of coffee or after a standing team meeting. However, if the individual's opposition remains after you've made reasonable efforts to address it, ask the executive sponsor to intervene prior to the event. In rare cases, the team might need to remove an employee from the tabletop exercise. While this is a drastic measure, a participant actively opposing the tabletop during the actual event could throw the exercise into disarray.

Outsourcing Tabletop Exercises

As the complexity of the information technology landscape has grown, many organizations now outsource their cybersecurity needs to remote services such as vCISOs and SOCs. Tabletop exercises are just one of many cybersecurity activities that an organization can outsource to a trusted vendor.

Many organizations lack a large enough information security budget to bring in an external consultant, which can be costly. Tabletop exercises can range in price from $5,000 to $25,000 depending on the required planning, complexity, delivery mechanism, duration, reporting, and other factors. For some companies, the cost of bringing in an external party may be a nonstarter.

On the other hand, some organizations lack the necessary resources or knowledge to plan, develop, and facilitate such an event. It's quite possible that no staff member has ever participated in a tabletop exercise before, whether with their current employer or in a past career. By contrast, individual members of a consultancy firm may execute 30 or more tabletop exercises a year and have the know-how to navigate potential roadblocks or hurdles. As a compromise, some organizations hire an external facilitator but treat the development process as an opportunity to also cross-train an internal employee for the next exercise.

Consultancy firms also tend to have expertise in specific areas. For example, one consultancy firm may specialize in incident response and another in payment card industry compliance. These external vendors can answer questions such as "How are we doing compared to our peers?" An external vendor who is a veteran at facilitating a large number of tabletop exercises across numerous organizations and industry verticals provides invaluable knowledge.

In some organizations, there is a culture of looking to outside experts for guidance. In these cases, the organization may be more inclined to act upon recommendations of an external vendor, even if employees have made similar suggestions in the past. Those employees can use this to their advantage by having the external consultant advocate for important changes. For example, if an information security director has asked to implement multifactor authentication and been rebuffed, an external consultant can weave this issue into a tabletop exercise and list it as an identified deficiency.

Lastly, the outsourced tabletop exercise could serve as a *third-party assessment* meant to provide an unbiased point of view. (To remove as much residual bias as possible, choose a consultancy with few or no business connections with the organization.) Third-party assessments are a powerful tool, as observations and recommendations are unlikely to be clouded by conflicting interests. Also, external stakeholders evaluating an organization's information security posture may be suspicious of an internally conducted tabletop exercise that resulted in glowing reviews and few deficiencies. These third-party assessments are particularly salient to parties such as cyber insurance underwriters or auditors, who may even request copies of the documentation when assessing the risks of conducting business with the organization. Having proof of a tabletop exercise performed by a third party lends credibility to the report.

However, if you choose to outsource an exercise to a vendor, make sure to find the proper fit with the consultant assigned to the exercise. If, for example, a premier US art museum hired an external vendor to perform a tabletop exercise, and during their first meeting, the consultant said, "You guys have a bunch of painted canvases made by starving artists, right?" In doing so, the consultant demonstrated a lack of appreciation for the artwork, which was immensely important to museum staff. A consultant should be able to fit seamlessly into the organization, quickly understand the rungs on the organizational ladder, and not prompt a collective facepalm from the group.

If you're using an outside consultant to avoid dedicating too many internal resources to a tabletop exercise, be sure to ask about the consultant's development methodology, including how much time and what activities will be required of internal staff members. It's unlikely that they'll need to assemble the development team from the organization's staff, but a good consultant should solicit feedback from employees to ensure that the scenario they're developing is pertinent and meets the exercise's goals and objectives. If an outside consultant requires several hours of the organization's time to brainstorm scenarios, review deliverables, assist with revisions, and so on, the relationship may not realize the intended value, but someone showing up with a canned scenario that has nothing to do with the organization or its business may be even worse.

Summary

The activities in this chapter lay the foundation for a successful tabletop exercise and should help you hammer out the tabletop's format. Think about each of the considerations we've outlined here before moving on to the next chapter, where you'll develop the scenario for the exercise.

Questions

Most tabletop exercises require significant planning to be successful, so it's worth investing time and effort in the planning process. Start your tabletop development process on the right track by considering the following questions:

1. Who should be the tabletop exercise's executive sponsor? What important traits do they possess? Does this person exist at the right spot in the organizational chart?
2. What do you expect of your executive sponsor? Is the executive sponsor willing to perform these tasks?
3. What are your goals and objectives in performing the tabletop exercise?
4. Is this a senior-level or operational-level exercise?
5. Do you plan to perform a tandem tabletop exercise? If so, do you have the time to devote to additional planning and facilitation tasks?
6. Who must attend the tabletop exercise? Whose attendance is optional?
7. Who will perform the roles of development lead, facilitator, subject matter expert, and trusted agent?
8. Will the tabletop exercise be remote or in-person? If it's remote, what technology will you require for your event to succeed? If it's in-person, what logistical components should you consider?
9. How long will your tabletop exercise be?
10. How will you communicate about the event to attendees? Who will be responsible for this communication?
11. How will you allow attendees to ask questions? If you schedule discussion sessions, who will attend these sessions?
12. Do you anticipate any opposition to the tabletop exercise? If so, what is your plan to address it?
13. How will you maintain the confidentiality of the scenario?

3

THE DEVELOPMENT PROCESS: WHERE THE RUBBER MEETS THE ROAD

In this chapter, we focus on how the development team constructs its tabletop exercise, from defining a topic to creating the exercise materials. By the end, you'll have chosen a topic, crafted a scenario and injects, designed a storyboard and ground truth document, and assembled your presentation deck.

Depending on the particulars of each tabletop exercise, you might occasionally skip some of the steps outlined in this chapter. For example, the exercise topic might emerge quickly after a vice president tells you, "We need to practice our ability to respond to a business email compromise." Many tabletops are developed in this fashion; you'll know some of the initial components (such as the scope and topic) and fill in the rest (like duration and goals) based on what is already in place. As with each chapter, you should take stock of the organizational dynamics, business requirements, and unique threat landscape of your organization before you proceed.

Choosing a Topic

The tabletop exercise's *topic* is the overarching issue to explore. It could be an information security–related issue (such as ransomware, an insider threat, or phishing) or a disaster scenario impacting the organization's ability to respond to information security events (such as a hazardous train derailment or hurricane that prevents the organization's staff from being able to work). Ideally, you should choose a topic that your organization wants to prepare for and won't flummox exercise participants when revealed.

The specific topic isn't as important as you might believe, however, because you can take almost any topic in a variety of directions. For example, an exercise with ransomware as its topic could explore the lateral movement of the attacker (that is, how an attack spreads throughout a network), responses to regulatory entities, business continuity issues, or investigatory actions. You could just as easily explore those issues in exercises based on the topic of a nation-state attack or a vendor security failure.

The topic can be used as an opportunity to consider an area that piques participants' interest. If the organization has a certain issue on its radar, selecting a related topic could make the exercise especially salient to participants and other stakeholders. This section describes some tips for choosing the topic.

Consult Your Business Impact Analysis

If the organization has performed a *business impact analysis (BIA)*—a document outlining the possible business impact of various disruptions to business functions and processes—you can use it to help choose your tabletop exercise topic.

Granted, the BIA may focus on a wide spectrum of events, from natural disasters to civil unrest to supply chain interruptions; however, it also likely touches on cybersecurity issues, including ransomware, leaks of protected data (such as intellectual property and personally identifiable information, or PII), and loss of critical computing infrastructure. The BIA may also describe an entire scenario in which a cybersecurity event impacts the organization. If so, you could use this as your topic.

Leveraging the BIA for the tabletop exercise topic provides an opportunity to pull in yet another collaborator: the subject matter expert who spearheaded the BIA, whether their background is in disaster recovery, risk management, or another area. You can enlist this expert to briefly speak at the beginning of the tabletop exercise to explain that the topic was chosen because of its significant impact on the organization, reinforcing the exercise's importance.

Finally, many organizations have reflected on how to react to a natural disaster (such as an incoming hurricane or snowstorm) but neglected to plan for a cybersecurity incident that could have some of the same impacts. The tabletop exercise could be an opportunity for the business continuity or disaster recovery teams to collaborate with the information security teams to ensure that they consider cybersecurity events in the future.

Confer with the Executive Sponsor

Another way to find inspiration for the tabletop exercise is to confer with the executive sponsor. More likely than not, they have a particular cybersecurity concern in mind. And even if the topic you choose doesn't reflect the sponsor's individual interests, you should seek their feedback to ensure that they're supportive of and invested in the tabletop exercise topic; not having an executive sponsor supportive of your tabletop exercise topic is counterproductive and should be avoided.

Leverage Other Resources for Inspiration

Beyond the topic selection methods we've just listed, you could develop a relevant topic by:

- Asking executives about the cybersecurity concerns that keep them up at night
- Tracking and mining trends from governmental or industry sources for ideas
- Asking vendors involved in cybersecurity what issues they're seeing in the industry

Once you've settled on a topic, you can begin crafting the exercise's scenario.

Developing the Scenario

The *scenario* is the unique story that the tabletop exercise explores. For some tabletop exercises, selecting this scenario is a simple process. Perhaps there's an obvious choice inspired by an event in the news, a known security risk in the organization, a recent internal incident, or a management directive. In these situations, the development phase is likely to progress with smooth sailing.

However, you might enter into the tabletop exercise development without a specific scenario to explore. Maybe such exercises are new to the organization, or maybe the organization has performed so many tabletop exercises that it has exhausted obvious scenarios. Alternatively, maybe management has requested a tabletop exercise but hasn't provided parameters for the scenario. If you find yourself in this situation, rest assured that many development teams have faced this exact quandary.

Characteristics of an Effective Scenario

You shouldn't develop your scenario arbitrarily. As you learned in Chapter 2, it's not uncommon for someone in authority or the exercise participants themselves to ask about the chosen scenario prior to the exercise. If this happens, you should be able to articulate the factors that went into its development. In addition to being able to meet the goals and objectives of the exercise, the scenario should be:

- Realistic
- Relevant to both the organization and the participants
- An opportunity to examine known or potential weaknesses

Let's explore these guidelines further.

Keep Scenarios Realistic

While you can get creative with your exercise scenario, you don't have license to cross into the realm of fantasy. Participants may have to suspend a certain degree of disbelief, and a scenario may push the boundaries of what is plausible, but it should not be utterly absurd.

What makes for a realistic scenario? Try looking at real events for inspiration, including documented cyberattacks, organizational failures to properly respond to an incident, known malware, and insider attacks. You could then try ratcheting up pain points from these known attacks while still staying within the level of plausibility, although there's no shame in keeping it simple, too. Some of the best tabletops have been incredibly brief, as the examples provided in Part II of this book will demonstrate.

During the tabletop exercise, the facilitator may be put in the position of having to defend the scenario's viability. In these cases, they might find it useful to have statistics or brief case studies on hand to present to the audience. These statistics and examples should correspond to a specific inject and relate to the organization performing the exercise.

CASE STUDY: A FAR-FETCHED SCENARIO

Let's consider an example in which a tabletop exercise went sideways because of a far-fetched scenario. A large coffee chain, ColdBrew, wanted to perform an exercise after a recent string of cybersecurity incidents stemming from common failures in information security, including a lack of end-user awareness, poor password policies, and a failure to patch endpoints. The coffee chain had already implemented several improvements to its policies and processes. Next, its information security manager, James, hired an external tabletop facilitator to challenge the staff to think outside the box.

Although the external facilitator suggested a scenario based on the recent incidents, James opted for one that would "throw the staff for a loop." In the scenario, ColdBrew heard from several payment card providers that many of its stores had been sites of fraudulent transactions. The implicated stores used a point-of-sale (POS) system downloaded onto an iPad from the Apple App Store. Through its investigation, ColdBrew determined that attackers had uploaded a malicious version of the POS system to the iPads by compromising the cellular network, the primary method the iPads used to communicate with the internet.

The attackers had then intercepted updates sent to the POS system and installed the malicious version on ColdBrew's systems.

During the exercise, ColdBrew's CIO called the scenario preposterous, as it required a confluence of independent failure points, including in cellular networks and POS systems. These had no precedent and were highly unlikely, if not outright impossible. After making these comments, the CIO disengaged from the tabletop exercise. The other attendees took their cue from the CIO and checked out as well.

As you can see, when you push the bounds of reality, participants might lose motivation. If ColdBrew had opted for a scenario that reflected the organization's threat landscape, the participants might have been more engaged and received more value from the exercise.

Ensure Scenarios Are Relevant

While a *realistic* scenario is grounded in the realm of possibility, a *relevant* one is pertinent to the business. In other words, would the scenario elicit a collective "So what?" from participants if it were to occur?

Relevance is often best measured in terms of the scenario's business impact, so you need to be familiar with the organization's pain points. Your exercise doesn't have to target the most significant business impact, but you should focus on a scenario that is relevant enough to capture the attendees' attention. Let's examine a few:

- A fast-food restaurant relies on a software platform that processes drive-through orders. If the system were inaccessible due to a cybersecurity incident, the restaurant would have to take orders by hand, which would be slower, reducing the number of customers it could serve and significantly impacting sales.

- Over 80 percent of the purchases at a home improvement store use a credit card. The card payment terminals attached to the POS systems use a third-party vendor to authenticate the customers' credit cards. If the third-party vendor became inoperable for several days due to a cybersecurity attack, the business would suffer from an immediate loss of sales and diminished customer satisfaction.

- A commercial property in Arizona uses industrial-sized cooling systems, which contractors can log in to remotely to perform health checks. If the credentials became compromised and an attacker shut down the cooling system, the property would be quickly uninhabitable due to Arizona's desert climate.

In each of the examples, there is a clear business impact that would be impossible to ignore, capturing the attention of executives and customers alike.

Finally, make sure the executive sponsor agrees that the scenario is relevant. If at any point during the tabletop exercise the executive sponsor could be thinking, *So what?*, you should adjust the scenario.

**CASE STUDY: A TABLETOP EXERCISE
WITH A RELEVANT SCENARIO**

ElecNet, a specialty manufacturer of industrial electrical components, planned a tabletop exercise involving a compromise of the IT systems used to manufacture Atlas, its flagship product. Atlas was a mobile electric substation meant for use in disasters, such as after a tornado, when electrical substations have been destroyed. Using the Atlas system, a large trailer could connect to the power grid to provide emergency power to consumers.

However, when the development team discussed the scenario with the executive sponsor, the sponsor questioned its relevance. Most Atlas purchases happened during an emergency, which required ElecNet to have a sizable number of premade Atlas systems ready for delivery. As there were months' worth of Atlas systems available to ship, losing the manufacturing systems would be inconvenient but wouldn't create significant urgency. Also, even a catastrophic information security event would result in several weeks of manufacturing downtime at most, which wouldn't ultimately impact ElecNet's ability to fulfill customer orders because of the amount of Atlas systems ElecNet keeps on hand. In other words: so what?

The executive sponsor provided a more relevant suggestion. Because ElecNet claimed it could ship Atlas systems worldwide to most client sites within 24 hours, the IT systems that supported international customs clearances were far more critical than the manufacturing systems. And because approximately half of ElecNet's business was international, so were the systems that supported the cross-border transit of the devices. The inability to ship internationally, or any delays incurred by an incident, posed a significant risk to the organization and became the premise of the new scenario.

The scenario must be relevant to attendees, too, as they're committing a chunk of their day to it. For example, you could skew a ransomware tabletop toward members of the legal department by focusing on the regulatory concerns of paying a ransom; alternatively, you could focus on the technical attendees' ability to detect and contain the ransomware.

Ensure that none of the attendees have a reason to ask themselves, *Why am I here?* If you're unable to easily identify how a scenario relates to their roles, consider altering it to increase their engagement.

Highlight Known or Potential Weaknesses

An excellent strategy for making your exercise extra valuable is to choose a scenario that highlights a known or potential weakness in the organization's environment. Organizations often perform tabletop exercises following a cybersecurity incident as part of the "lessons learned" process, when they've shored up known deficiencies and want to determine whether there are residual shortcomings to address.

The organization's information security team may also be aware of a deficiency in their security practices, such as retaining important logs for only a few days. This may occur because the team has been unable to obtain funding to store logs for a longer duration. The exercise provides an opportunity to explore the impact of the deficiency during a cybersecurity incident response. Playing out the scenario in front of leadership might prompt the organization to address the weakness and secure additional funding.

**CASE STUDY: A SCENARIO THAT EXPLORES
KNOWN WEAKNESSES**

The newly appointed information security officer at a bank was concerned about the threat of ransomware. However, when she asked leaders if the bank would entertain paying a ransom, their answers were often contradictory: the CEO emphatically stated "Never"; the chief legal officer said, "Maybe, depending on the situation"; and the CISO believed that paying the ransom would be the only viable option. The information security officer knew that she needed clarity on the bank's response in such an event; any indecision would prolong the incident response process and hinder recovery efforts.

To address these discrepancies, the information security officer used a tabletop exercise to bring together the bank's leadership. In the scenario she developed, ransomware entered the bank's environment, the backups became corrupted, and the only option to quickly return to business was to pay the attacker. The conversation during the tabletop exercise revealed a lack of agreement that, in the event of a real ransomware attack, would only delay the bank's response—a fact that the participants acknowledged.

The tabletop provided the forum for all parties to come together and discuss what would happen if the bank were facing a similar situation and to coalesce around a plan of action. By the end of the tabletop exercise, the information security officer better understood leadership's preferences when it came to paying the ransom—a result that would save valuable time in the organization's response to an actual incident.

Sources of Inspiration for Your Scenario

In addition to ensuring the scenario is both realistic and relevant, you can seek internal or external sources of inspiration for the scenario. Perhaps the organization has conducted previous assessments that highlighted deficiencies within its processes. Or perhaps the FBI and CISA have just released a new joint Cybersecurity Advisory highlighting a new ransomware variant.

Let's explore some of these inspiration sources further.

Review Previous Assessments

You can find inspiration for your scenario by looking back to previous assessment activities, such as penetration tests or prior tabletops. These activities should have yielded a report documenting any deficiencies, which you can use to inform your scenario. Using previous assessment activities as your inspiration adds credence to the selected scenario, as it has already been shown to be plausible and to have a demonstrable impact on the organization.

Finally, incorporating an existing security gap into your scenario will likely garner additional support from the organization as a whole or from select members who have an interest in addressing that deficiency. For example, if a prior penetration test revealed that a server was using an antiquated software package with known vulnerabilities, but the business unit resisted risk management's calls to address it, weaving these details into a scenario will likely earn support from the risk management team for the tabletop exercise.

Turn to External Resources

If real-world examples or prior cybersecurity events don't help you settle on a relevant and realistic scenario, consider drawing inspiration from the following free or cost-effective resources:

The Cybersecurity and Infrastructure Security Agency (CISA)

CISA provides scenarios along with corresponding materials at *https:// www.cisa.gov/cisa-tabletop-exercise-packages*. Even if the scenarios don't exactly align with your requirements, the materials may offer a baseline that you can alter as needed.

Your cyber insurance provider

As a party with a vested interest in reducing the risk faced by the organization, your insurer may be able to offer input on which scenarios would be most beneficial in a tabletop exercise.

Law enforcement sources

Law enforcement agencies can describe the threat landscape they observe when responding to criminal matters. Public-private partnerships—such as InfraGard, which serves as a bridge between the FBI and the public sector—enable access to law enforcement professionals. Drawing upon these relationships can provide inspiration based on real-world events.

Peers in the cybersecurity industry or in the same industry vertical

Industry peers are usually happy to exchange information regarding the threat landscape, provided it doesn't compromise any confidentiality agreements. While reaching out to your contacts is an excellent starting point, you can cast a wider net by posting in LinkedIn groups or other public forums. However, be aware of confidentiality issues when doing so; stating that your organization is performing a tabletop exercise on ransomware because "we just aren't ready and are a sitting duck for an attack" is fodder for a threat actor. Also keep in mind that this kind of outreach might not be acceptable for some organizations.

SEC Form 10-K (if the organization is publicly traded)

This form—which an organization files to inform shareholders of risk factors it faces (among other items)—is likely to include specific cybersecurity risks, as most organizations recognize the threat posed by cybersecurity attacks.

With the topic and scenario roughly defined, it's now time to consider the components of the tabletop exercise that you'll present to participants via injects.

Introducing Injects

An *inject* is a set of facts presented during the tabletop exercise to convey new information or bring clarity to information previously provided. The inject may also add temporal details, such as the date and time, to artificially move the scenario to some point in the future. It can be as simple as a few bullet points and is intended to help the facilitator guide the scenario and keep participants focused on select areas of the response. It's helpful to think of an inject as someone coming into your office and telling you what they just discovered.

Let's consider a few examples. Figure 3-1 shows an inject for a technical exercise involving data exfiltration from a bank's SQL server containing sensitive financial data.

Inject 1: Technical Exercise

Monday 7:20 AM CST

- The MSSP calls to report that it has seen a large data transfer from the network to an IP address associated with a known threat actor.
- The internal IP address associated with the alert is the core banking SQL server, which hosts all customer account information, including bank account numbers, addresses, and social security numbers.

Old Prairie BANK

Figure 3-1: An inject slide for a sample tabletop exercise

During this inject, participants could discuss the technical aspects of the response, such as gathering intelligence on the destination IP, reviewing the SQL server to determine what data was accessed, and reviewing the environment for other systems the threat actor may have compromised.

Figure 3-2 shifts the focus to the executive leadership's involvement in an extortion demand from a threat actor who purportedly exported 150GB of data from the environment.

Inject 2: Executive Exercise

Monday 8:35 AM CST

- The threat actor sends a message to the CEO.
- The threat actor indicates that 150GB of data has been exfiltrated, which includes customer information.
- The threat actor demands payment of 25 Bitcoin within 48 hours or the amount will double. After an additional 48 hours, the data will be put up for sale on the dark web.

Old Prairie BANK

Figure 3-2: A leadership-focused inject for a sample tabletop exercise

During such an inject, we'd expect leadership to discuss the impact of the ransom demand, whether to pay the ransom, the internal and external communications required, and how to validate that the data exfiltrated is, in fact, customer data.

Finally, Figure 3-3 shows an inject to prompt several teams—including information security, information technology, and physical security (at a minimum)—to get involved in the response.

Inject 3: Physical Security Example

Monday 9:50 AM CST

- While investigating the physical server in the data center, the server admin finds an unknown device plugged into the back of the server.
- Physical Security is alerted, and access control logs are requested along with video camera feeds from the cameras inside and outside the data center.

Old Prairie BANK

Figure 3-3: An inject to involve nontechnical teams in a sample tabletop exercise

To respond to this inject, physical security would need to play a major role by determining who had access to the data center at the time that the device was installed, including discussing how long they maintain video footage and access logs. Additionally, information technology and information security would discuss their role and the process of investigating the unknown device.

Simulate Time Constraints

Injects also enable your exercise to explore, in just a few hours, an incident that may last for weeks or months. You can use injects to insert new information, letting the scenario quickly evolve as it might play out in real time.

During a complex cybersecurity incident, the organization rarely understands the full extent of the situation right away. It can often take days, weeks, or even months for all parties to get a complete picture of what took place. The initial hours and days of an incident are likely to be filled with bits and pieces of information; confusion abounds, and the best course of action is debatable. Injects are especially helpful for simulating these conditions because they can introduce doubt and confusion into the exercise using controlled information, then explore the incident within the time allotted.

Direct Focus

Another reason injects are helpful is that they direct the development team to focus on particular aspects of the organization's response to a cybersecurity incident. For example, if one objective of a tabletop exercise is to focus on how the organization interacts with the media after a very public and high-profile incident, an inject can introduce a set of facts that steer participants toward addressing that topic. For example, halfway through a tabletop exercise for a medical billing company that has so far focused on business continuity issues, the facilitator might use an inject like the one shown in Figure 3-4.

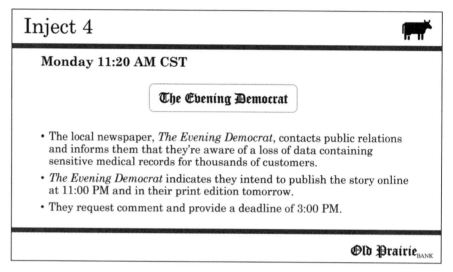

Figure 3-4: A media-involved inject

Now the group must shift its focus to examining existing processes for communicating with the media, such as who performs the communications, whether the legal team must approve statements, and whether to call in a public relations expert for assistance. An inject is no different from a person running into a conference room filled with incident responders and shouting, "Guys! The media just called! They want a statement by 3 PM!" In a tabletop exercise, you can provide the same information in a controlled fashion with a predefined inject and a low-stress environment in which to discuss the response.

Finally, injects with a specific focus also enable you to ensure that select attendees are included in the discussion. While the inject in Figure 3-4 focuses on issues pertaining to communications and media, another inject could easily focus on physical security, vendor management, or human resources. Because of the narrow focus, it is important that the development team invite a representative who can address the particular discipline reflected in the inject.

Balance Clarity and Conciseness

How many injects are appropriate for a tabletop exercise? As always, it depends, but here are a few factors to consider:

- For a two-hour tabletop exercise, 7 to 10 injects should be enough to provide a coherent story arc that enables the group to explore a variety of topics.

- More injects aren't necessarily better. The more complicated the tabletop exercise becomes, the less concise and focused the scenario. Also, when a scenario becomes too wide reaching, attendees can be overwhelmed by the number of issues to address. Exploring a few key themes in depth can be more beneficial than scratching the surface of too many.

- Depending on the attendees' culture of participation, some tabletop exercises require only a small number of injects, such as three (the minimum needed to present introductory information, a new piece of information, and a final wrap-up). An especially chatty group with only a few injects can easily consume 90 minutes of discussion.

- If the tabletop exercise is allotted a two-hour block, aim to go short versus long. A tabletop exercise that finishes with time remaining enables participants to complete the scenario without feeling rushed.

- A tabletop exercise that runs long can cause schedule conflicts for attendees, some of whom may be higher-profile executives with already limited availability.

- Most tabletop exercises benefit from a question-and-answer session at the end; jamming in too many injects may inhibit this benefit. Because one goal of a tabletop exercise is to develop relationships, setting aside time at the end of the session to discuss leftover topics that emerged or other general concerns can make the event more valuable.

Injects must strike a balance between adding clarity, fostering collaboration between attendees, and creating some ambiguity about which next steps to take. That said, they shouldn't bog down participants with too many options. Sometimes, the most effective injects have just a few bullets and less than 20 words on a slide. Avoid injects that look like a doctoral dissertation written in 8-point font that take several minutes for participants to fully digest. If you find yourself throwing the kitchen sink at attendees with a single inject, consider breaking the inject into logical segments.

Designing the Exercise Storyboard

The general concept of your tabletop exercise is starting to come alive. After some mental thrashing, you've defined goals and chosen a topic through which to explore cybersecurity issues. You've developed a scenario and identified participants. Now you go off and build it, right?

As with most activities in life, even after an idea takes shape, you may find that you have to pivot. The threat landscape might have changed (for example, if a new attack appears in the news), or an executive sponsor might ask you to reorient your scenario toward another priority. Sometimes to the frustration of the development team, a tabletop exercise might undergo several modifications prior to delivery. This is where storyboarding comes into play. This practice originated in the film industry as an efficient way to solidify a movie's plot and aesthetics prior to its production.

Applied to tabletop exercises, the concept is no different: *storyboarding* is simply making a rough draft of the exercise that you can easily alter if desired. It enables the development team to choreograph the scenario without investing too much time into the process. At this stage, it's easy to make modifications. With a storyboard, the development team can visualize how the tabletop exercise will play out and identify avenues for improvement or potential pitfalls.

Storyboards do not need to be formal. A few members of the development team can quickly sketch one out on a whiteboard. Include a brief description of the injects (one or two sentences is sufficient) and the key issues each inject is intended to explore. The development team can take a step back, review the storyboard, and ask themselves, "Does this make sense?" Also, an outsider reviewing the storyboard should be able to quickly follow the overall theme and understand what you're trying to accomplish.

Tabletops frequently follow the structure of NIST's incident response lifecycle, depicted in Figure 3-5, which starts with preparation; breaks down incident response into detection and analysis, as well as containment, eradication, and recovery; and eventually leads to post-incident activity. Tabletop exercises don't need to explicitly contain the preparation phase, as this stage comprises the tabletop itself and related planning activities.

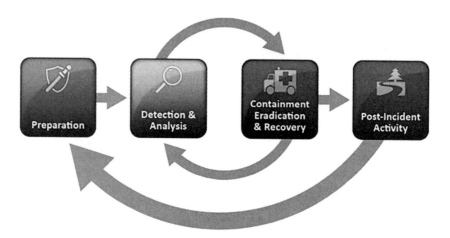

Figure 3-5: The NIST incident response lifecycle

For example, most tabletop exercises and real-life cybersecurity incidents start with a simple event: a system administrator recognizing an unusual account with escalated privileges, a network appliance firing off an alert after a security rule is tripped, or a law enforcement agency knocking on the door to notify the organization that its data may have been stolen, to name a few. This catalyzing event must be defined during storyboard development and kicks off the tabletop exercise. (We'll talk more about this in "Considering the Scenario Escalation Pace" on page 67.)

Once the initial information is presented, new information steadily trickles in via injects, bringing clarity to the scenario without revealing too much information at any one time. Starting slowly keeps the discussion focused on one intended area. Additional injects can add detail to the scenario in future stages, such as containment or recovery efforts, and eventually into a "lessons learned" debrief activity. You can see this process unfold in the following example storyboard.

STORYBOARD: MALWARE DISCOVERY

A system administrator for Modern Health Technology Solutions (MHTS), an IT outsourcing company that supports small-to-medium pharmacies with their IT needs, discovers a server consuming a large percentage of CPU resources. Upon further inspection, the sysadmin locates an unknown piece of software, named *BS87AB.EXE*, on the server. Based on an MD5 hash value and initial research in the information security community, the sysadmin suspects that the file is malicious.

Key Issues

- Per the organization's processes, is this a cybersecurity incident?
- Is there a process through which the sysadmin can escalate this incident to parties with a need to know? If so, is the sysadmin aware of the process?
- Is the sysadmin empowered to perform containment measures (such as shutting down a system)?

INJECT 1

MHTS's network administrators examine network logs and determine that a large data set, well over 50GB, was sent from the server to an IP address associated with criminal activity.

Key Issues

- How many days of network logs are available for network administrators to examine?
- Would current logging standards record the network traffic? What limitations in logging might inhibit the analysis?
- Is it possible to determine what data was exfiltrated?
- Would MHTS immediately know what data is processed or stored by the server?
- At this point, who oversees the investigation?

(continued)

INJECT 2

The MHTS information security team examines the server and determines that (a) there was a misconfigured account with a default password, (b) logins from foreign and unknown IP addresses had been occurring for the past six months, and (c) with access to the misconfigured account, an attacker had the potential to access other systems in MHTS.

Key Issues

- Can MHTS quickly determine whether there are misconfigured accounts on other systems?
- Is it possible to determine whether lateral movement occurred?
- If lateral movement did occur, is it possible to determine what systems were accessed?

INJECT 3

MHTS discovers that the attacker had access to several systems containing protected health information (PHI) belonging to both customers and employees.

Key Issues

- Is it possible to determine what specific records were accessed?
- Is MHTS able to quickly determine what data is on each system that was accessed?
- How can MHTS determine whether the data's integrity has been maintained?
- Was any of the exfiltrated data PHI?
- If PHI has been impacted, do additional parties in MHTS need to be notified?

INJECT 4

Analysis has revealed several indicators of compromise (IoCs) consisting of a change to the Windows registry, IP addresses, and MD5 hash values of suspicious files. If a system within MHTS is found to contain any of these IoCs, it is highly likely that it has been accessed by the attacker.

Key Issues

- With this investigatory data, is it possible to quickly determine whether any systems in MHTS contain these IoCs?
- Is MHTS able to create rules that notify MHTS staff if the IoCs appear elsewhere on the network?

INJECT 5

The IoCs reveal that a foreign party logged in to a new server just one hour before. The server is an important system responsible for distributing flu vaccinations to pharmacies throughout the East Coast. The business continuity team is consulted; it reports that because the server is used only seasonally, it wasn't included in the business continuity planning. It will take at least a week to bring an alternative online.

Key Issues

- Does MHTS information security and information technology staff have a clear understanding of what tasks each system performs?

- If there is a clear justification, is MHTS staff authorized to shut down a system performing the distribution of flu vaccines, a high-availability system that impacts patient health? If not, who has this authority?

The storyboard is concise, and writing an initial draft should take only about an hour. Any party can quickly understand its overarching theme, the injects that will add nuance, and the key issues to bring up during the discussion. An even more concise storyboard could omit the "Key Issues" sections; however, these help the reader understand the justification for each inject.

Now say the development team wants to adjust the exercise so it includes a unique threat vector, such as an individual outside an MHTS facility breaking into its networks via wireless connections. Making such a course correction while storyboarding is easy to accomplish and wouldn't impact polished content, such as a PowerPoint deck.

Another benefit of storyboarding is that it enables the development team to provide a rough blueprint to select stakeholders, particularly the executive sponsor, to ensure their buy-in. The tabletop exercise has now evolved from theoretical discussions to a practical draft; especially if you're a consultant, you can document that the client's points of contact have weighed in on the scenario and voiced their approval.

Considering the Scenario Escalation Pace

When storyboarding and planning your injects, give some thought to the overall escalation pace of the scenario and what is appropriate for the tabletop exercise. The *escalation pace* refers to the severity of the information being introduced at each inject. In many real-world incident response scenarios, there's an initial catalyst that may seem relatively benign:

- An end user contacts the help desk because their computer is running slow.

- A network administrator observes unexpected spikes in network traffic in the middle of the night when no one is working.
- An end user loses their laptop at the airport.

Each of these examples is worthy of further exploration and could easily become more serious as additional details emerge. In fact, there are plenty of well-known cybersecurity incidents that started with simple events similar to these, only to balloon into a far bigger problem. By starting slowly and building up to a more severe incident, attendees are able to explore how the organization would respond to the initial indicators of a potential threat. As an ancillary benefit, if a participant is attending a tabletop exercise for the first time, this approach eases them into the exercise.

Providing a more consequential set of facts for the initial inject can be appropriate for some tabletop exercises; however, consider whether forgoing the slow buildup to a more severe incident sacrifices a salient exploration of how the organization would respond to indicators of a bigger threat.

Crafting Your Ground Truth Document

Once you've agreed on a rough storyboard, it's time to craft the ground truth document. The United States' Homeland Security Exercise and Evaluation Program (HSEEP) defines a *ground truth document* as follows:

> A document comprised of the detailed elements of a scenario that must remain consistent during exercise development [. . .] to ensure that realism is maintained, and objectives can be achieved.

Whereas the storyboard is an informal sketch that helps you brainstorm the scenario, the ground truth formalizes the tabletop exercise, developing the backstory and defining the injects.

A ground truth document may not always be necessary. For example, if the organization's objective is merely getting stakeholders in the room to walk through how a cybersecurity incident would play out, it may be an extraneous formality. Likewise, if the organization wants to conduct a series of quick tabletop exercises over lunch, a ground truth document could be viewed as an unnecessary investment that makes the entire event cumbersome. Finally, a ground truth document may be impractical for tabletop exercises that are exploring situations where the organization may not have defined policies and procedures, as finding the right answer isn't as relevant as the discussion itself.

On the other hand, ground truth documents provide structure to the tabletop exercise development process. If the organization wants to implement a tabletop exercise program to regularly evaluate its level of maturity, the ground truth document can demonstrate the program's existence to auditors, vendors, and other external parties.

Perhaps the most important benefit of creating a ground truth document is that it can shorten the development process by enabling the development team to fully explore the tabletop's initial flow as defined in the storyboard. This exploration may reveal inadequacies, such as misaligned goals and objectives, technical or process gaps in the scenario that strain credulity, or other aspects that give the development team pause. With the ground truth document, you can reorient without having to waste time changing polished materials, such as a PowerPoint deck.

Using the definition from HSEEP, let's go over some guidelines for crafting a successful ground truth document.

Add Details and Expected Outcomes

While the storyboard provides a very cursory summary of the scenario, the ground truth document is an opportunity to dig into its specific elements. For example, in a storyboard, it would be sufficient to state the following in an inject:

> Ransomware enters the environment and encrypts information systems used by the human resources department. Prior to encrypting it, the threat actors exfiltrated data from key systems.

A ground truth document should contain a greater degree of specificity:

> The director of human resources, Stephen Rosenwald, receives a malicious email from *MissingPackage@FredEx.com* and clicks the link contained within it. The link downloads a PDF titled *MISSINGPACKAGE.PDF*, which Rosenwald also clicks.

> Rosenwald had recently complained about an endpoint security agent consuming system resources, and due to his senior-level position in the organization, the help desk had removed the agent from his system, inhibiting security controls. Furthermore, Rosenwald has administrator access, as is the norm within his company for executives.

> Due to the inhibited security controls, when Rosenwald opened the PDF, a variant of the $SomeBot malware family was able to execute, harvest credentials, and allow a foreign actor to connect to the server using Remote Desktop Protocol. The attacker was able to remotely connect to Rosenwald's account, which had access to the human resources database containing resumes, employee data, and health insurance options.

As you can see, the storyboard is a compressed, high-level version of what will become the inject, whereas the ground truth is more detailed. The ground truth document also often contains expected outcomes or definitions of success to highlight areas that the participants should address during the exercise. (You'll see sample definitions of success in the "Ground Truth: Malware Discovery" box on the following page.)

While not a complete exploration of the technical and organizational factors that led to the cybersecurity incident, the second paragraph contains details that would likely emerge during a tabletop exercise. This may readily address basic questions that participants will immediately ask. With this greater clarity, participants can understand how an incident occurred and what data was accessed, and they can start to assess the significance of the provided information.

Keep in mind that the detailed elements to include will vary based on the audience. If a highly technical audience is expected to participate in the tabletop exercise, the ground truth document should be a technical document written to cover as many technical details as possible that will be discussed. For senior-level tabletop exercises with cross-functional (such as nontechnical) audiences, in-depth technical details are unnecessary.

Maintain Realism

The ground truth document is another opportunity to ensure that the scenario stays realistic. Tabletop exercises should examine hypothetical—not farcical—events that the organization might face, and the ground truth document allows the development team to work through the details of a scenario from beginning to end, continually checking that it doesn't stray too far from the plausible.

Align with Objectives

The ground truth document should also consistently check that the tabletop exercise aligns with the objectives outlined at the onset of the development process. For example, say a primary objective is to test the organization's ability to effectively manage both public-facing and internal communications. When reviewing the ground truth, the development team may realize that the scenario focuses too heavily on technical factors and business continuity issues and doesn't prompt a natural exploration of communication tasks. Discovering this mismatch lets them reorient the scenario prior to the exercise.

GROUND TRUTH: MALWARE DISCOVERY

This ground truth document builds on the MHTS malware discovery storyboard. Note that it contains only the initial incident information and Inject 1 from the prior storyboard.

GOALS

Rehearse the incident response plan and malware infection playbook to identify any gaps in roles, responsibilities, and internal and external communications.

OBJECTIVES

- Ensure that proper communication and escalation procedures are defined within the incident response plan, known by the appropriate individuals, and followed during the tabletop exercise.
- Review core roles and responsibilities during a malware outbreak, ensuring that all involved personnel know what their role is during a similar incident.
- Ensure knowledge of the underlying tools and processes used during a malware outbreak.

AGENDA

11:00 AM: Introductions

11:10 AM: Goals and Objectives

11:15 AM: Tabletop Intro

11:30 AM: Inject 1

11:50 AM: Inject 2

12:10 PM: Lunch

12:40 PM: Inject 3

1:00 PM: Inject 4

1:20 PM: Inject 5

1:45 PM: Debrief

OVERVIEW

In October, HealthCare Plus Inc. announced an update to its core application, HCP Triage. Released nine months prior, the app's original version enabled a public-facing administrator account by default, which violated security norms. HCP Gold documentation widely available on the internet included the default administrator credentials. The October update aimed to rectify this information security shortcoming and remove the default administrator account.

Modern Health Technology Solutions (MHTS) is a medical provider using the HCP Triage program. Six months prior to the vulnerability's discovery, a threat actor used the administrator account to access the information stored on MHTS's instance of HCP Triage, as well as other MHTS systems. The attacker then silently monitored the environment to determine which systems contained sensitive information.

During those six months, the threat actor used the misconfigured account to access multiple systems and slowly exfiltrate data over port 3392/TCP using SSH. Additionally, they installed a backdoor on several systems to allow access back into the environment without account credentials.

(continued)

INTRODUCTION

A system administrator discovers a server consuming a large percentage of CPU resources and, upon further inspection, locates an unknown piece of software, named *BS87AB.EXE*, on the server. Based on an MD5 hash value and initial research in the information security community, the sysadmin suspects that the file is malicious. The information security team is notified of this activity via their preferred communication mechanism, *infosec@mhts.net*.

Key Issues

- Per the organization's processes, is this a cybersecurity incident?
- How long will it take before information security reviews the email received?
- Is there a process through which the sysadmin can escalate this incident to parties with a need to know? If so, is the sysadmin aware of the process?
- Is the sysadmin empowered to perform containment measures (such as shutting down a system)?

Definitions of Success

- Based on MHTS's Cybersecurity Incident Response Plan definition, this would be considered an incident because a suspected piece of malware has been found on an MHTS asset.
- Based on the information security team's standard operating procedure, emailed reports should be reviewed within 15 minutes.
- The sysadmin should immediately inform the incident manager of the situation (via phone and email) and ensure the incident manager acknowledges the reported incident. The incident manager will notify the necessary parties based on the known information. This process is outlined in the Cybersecurity Incident Response Plan.
- The sysadmin is empowered to perform containment activities on any systems not categorized as critical, which is defined in the Cybersecurity Incident Response Plan.

INJECT 1

MHTS's network administrators examine network logs and determine that a large amount of data, well over 50GB, was sent from the server to an IP address associated with criminal activity. Open source intelligence of the destination IP address reveals that the threat actor is known to sell stolen data on the dark web.

Key Issues

- How can we investigate the IP address to obtain information about the destination, and who is responsible for doing so?
- How many days of network logs are available for network administrators to examine?

- Would current logging standards record the network traffic? What limitations in logging may inhibit the analysis?
- Is it possible to determine what data was exfiltrated?
- At this point, who is in charge of the investigation?

Definitions of Success

- The network administrators are responsible for investigating logs relating to the IP address, under the direction of the incident manager.
- The Information Security Policy states that all logs are maintained for 90 days. Based on this and the fact that the incident likely started six months ago, there's a large gap in logging that may hinder analysis.
- Again, per the policy, the data should be available for 90 days within the security information and event management (SIEM) system. The relevant traffic may be discovered in NetFlow data, which is sent to the SIEM, and the response team would need to investigate whether the traffic is available. Given the age of the incident, the relevant data may no longer exist.
- This will require further investigative work and cannot be confirmed at this time; however, the incident response team should have several artifacts to examine in order to make this determination.
- Based on the Cybersecurity Incident Response Plan, the incident manager is in charge of the investigation.

As you can see in this example, the ground truth document builds upon the storyboard and adds further details to define the background of the incident being interrogated. It includes goals and objectives, exercise timing, greater detail in the injects, and expected outcomes.

Creating the Presentation Deck

With the storyboard complete and the ground truth settled, you can now focus on the deliverable for the tabletop exercise, which is often a slide deck created in the presentation software of your choice. This is the time to let your creative juices run wild.

While there is no one correct method to approach a presentation deck for a tabletop exercise, this section will provide a series of recommendations for its format and flow, as well as the critical components to cover. Most tabletop exercise presentation decks are broken into the following sections:

- Introductions
- Preamble
- Injects and Exercise Discussions
- Debrief

Some tabletop exercises also include an educational component, such as a short briefing on current trends in the threat landscape (for example, highlighting an uptick in phishing email). Even better, you could highlight security trends distilled from the organization itself; these are especially poignant, as they are relevant to the room.

Additionally, because the assembled group likely consists of members from the incident response team, the gathering could provide a forum for briefly discussing changes to the incident response plan, as well as the roles and responsibilities of participants. This refresher (which, for employees new to the incident response team, may really be more than a refresher) comes at the perfect time, as the group can then apply the material to the tabletop exercise.

Introductions

The introductions section of the presentation deck should contain basic information about the facilitator and their relationship to the organization. If the facilitator is an employee, you might not need to include their credentials, employment history, and so on, but if an outside contractor is facilitating, this background may be helpful to reinforce the breadth of their industry experience (and perhaps show that this isn't their first tabletop exercise).

Following the facilitator's introduction, set aside time for participants to introduce themselves. Often, participants will at least know each other's names and functions, but it's not uncommon for team members to be meeting each other for the first time during the tabletop exercises. Because these exercises are performed in part to ensure that all participants are familiar with each other's roles and responsibilities, time spent on introductions is worthwhile.

Dedicate no more than two or three slides to introductions. Depending on the size of the group and relationships between attendees, 5 to 10 minutes should suffice.

The Preamble

The facilitator should cover several topics in the preamble, including the purpose of tabletop exercises, proper etiquette, the importance of participation, and the expected outcome. The facilitator should also introduce the concept of injects. If this is the organization's first exercise, or if there are many first-time participants, setting an expectation prior to moving into the actual scenario can ensure that all participants are on the same page.

If the executive sponsor is attending the tabletop exercise, the preamble is an opportunity for them to say a few words that reinforce the importance of the exercise, thank everyone for participating, and emphasize that they're looking forward to understanding how the organization can improve after identifying gaps. The executive sponsor might also provide these words of encouragement during the introduction.

Be mindful that the elements of the preamble have the potential to steal precious time from the exercise itself. Ideally, the preamble should take no more than 15 minutes, leaving the bulk of the allotted time to the exercise.

Let's look at the components of the preamble in more detail.

Define the Rationale for the Exercise

It's very possible that several participants are questioning the value of performing a tabletop exercise. A brief slide and a few words from the facilitator can highlight its benefits, as you can see in Figure 3-6.

Why Perform Tabletop Exercises?

The media is full of stories about organizations experiencing cybersecurity incidents. We want to be ready when (not if) this happens to us.

We are here today to:

- Help prepare the organization for a cybersecurity incident.
- Identify gaps or deficiencies in people, processes, and technology related to incident response.
- Educate participants on their roles during a cybersecurity incident.

Old Prairie~BANK~

Figure 3-6: A slide explaining the purpose of a tabletop exercise

At a minimum, the slide should clarify that tabletop exercises help prepare the organization for a cybersecurity incident, identify gaps in existing processes, and educate response team members about their roles during a cybersecurity incident.

Establish Proper Etiquette for the Tabletop

Dedicate a slide or two to tabletop exercise etiquette. There's a good chance that participants are wondering what to expect over the next two hours. Will it be adversarial? How can they contribute? What is expected of them? These are fair questions and may generate a certain amount of confusion.

It's also very possible that a participant may want to defend an organization from the weaknesses presented in the scenario. Put yourself in the shoes of a system administrator hearing, in a tabletop exercise, that an internet-facing system had services enabled with default usernames and passwords. The sysadmin might immediately jump in to explain how there are policies, system build processes, regular external penetration testing, and other various checks to prevent such a situation from occurring.

The facilitator can avoid some of this defensive behavior by taking the time to briefly discuss how the scenario was developed. This can help eliminate the perception that it was created by an overcaffeinated risk management professional letting their imagination run wild. A slide such as the one in Figure 3-7 can help head off objections and speculation about the development process.

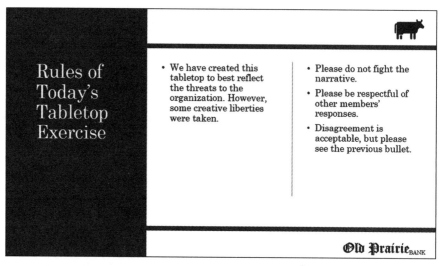

Figure 3-7: A slide introducing tabletop etiquette for a sample exercise

This slide emphasizes that this tabletop exercise has taken some creative liberties and asks participants not to fight the narrative. Acknowledging these two points should reduce or eliminate resistance when participants start to process the scenario.

Encourage Participation

It is also important to request that all attendees participate in the discussions. Tabletops are most effective when a large number of participants are engaged, contribute points and counterpoints, and tactfully question decisions or processes.

Encourage each attendee to discuss their *individual* interests or those related to their function. For example, representatives from legal may have very different concerns than those from business continuity. Consider the following brief exchange between representatives from information security and finance regarding calling a vendor for emergency support:

Information security: If it became that bad, we would just call in our vendor for incident response support.

Finance: Wait, do we have contracts in place with the vendor? I thought we let the contract lapse. And what will that run us?

Information security: We would have to get them signed quickly. And it won't be cheap. I would be surprised if we got away with anything less than a $50,000 bill.

Finance: Obviously, if we need to pull them in, then we need to pull them in. But we have a hard-and-fast policy that all contracts over $25,000 need to be reviewed by legal and procurement. I have never seen a review escape legal faster than 48 hours.

Clearly, both information security and finance have the same goal: to address a cybersecurity incident. However, they each bring up salient points relevant to their individual functions, enabling the other party to understand potential hurdles they would need to confront during an incident.

A slide like the one in Figure 3-8 can help foster the spirit of participation.

Participation Is Encouraged

- This exercise won't succeed unless you each participate.
- When an inject relates to an area for which you are responsible, please speak up.
- There are no right or wrong answers.
- Even if you are not responsible for the response to a given inject, feel free to provide your opinion.

Old PrairieBANK

Figure 3-8: A slide encouraging participation in a sample tabletop exercise

A tabletop in which few attendees speak will only cause a malaise to slowly fill the room, diminishing the value of the event.

Convey Intended Outcomes

Prior to digging into the scenario, all participants should understand the intended output of the tabletop exercise. You can accomplish this with a short slide and accompanying discussion (Figure 3-9).

Goal and Objectives

Goal:

- Conduct the organization's first ever tabletop exercise.

Important:

Participants are not being graded or evaluated.

Objectives:

- Build relationships within the incident response team.
- Understand individual and team roles during a cybersecurity incident.
- Provide a written report of key areas for improvement.

Figure 3-9: A slide discussing expected outcomes for a sample tabletop exercise

Most often, the output of a tabletop is a report listing recommendations and identified opportunities for improvement. These may range from recognizing that key stakeholders weren't notified in a timely manner to addressing a lack of clarity over what resources are available to the organization via its cyber insurance policy. Chapter 5 covers the specifics of reporting.

Potentially most important is describing to participants what *won't* happen. Even if you assured them otherwise before the exercise, some attendees may still believe that they're being personally evaluated, causing them to be overly defensive or withdrawn. For example, if management has indicated that certain business units are a financial drain or lower priority, an attendee from one of these groups may feel the need to grandstand to demonstrate their value. Thus, emphasize before starting that the goal of the tabletop exercise is not to evaluate individual responses and that you won't assign grades or point out individual failures.

Before moving on, make sure that participants don't have any lingering questions. Once those are addressed, you're ready to begin the exercise.

Injects and Exercise Discussions

With the etiquette and ground rules covered, you can now design the core portion of the tabletop: the inject slides. If you've developed a storyboard or ground truth document, you can easily identify the number of slides you'll need to convey the events of the incident.

We recommend including the following components on each inject slide:

Date and timestamps   These show the timing of the particular inject.

The injects   In some cases, you will want to display all information on the slide at once, whereas for other scenarios you may wish to reveal certain details as the discussion unfolds. As previously mentioned, this should be as short as possible, not a dissertation.

Imagery   While you won't always need an image to tell the story, graphics can often communicate details. As an example, for a ransomware-based scenario, adding a doctored ransom note from an actual ransomware variant can be an eye-opener.

Optionally, and helpful for a novice facilitator, you can follow up each inject slide with prewritten questions to keep the tabletop exercise on track. Consider the inject and its prewritten questions in the following box.

INJECT

A media representative from BSNews is inquiring about a PII data leak affecting customer data and has requested comment prior to going on air during the 5 PM news segment.

Questions

- Would every employee who received a call from the news outlet know whom to direct the call to?
- Who is responsible for responding?
- What would be said?
- Do we have a prewritten template that can be used?

This example asks the participants to answer these questions while also elaborating on other response efforts related to media communications.

If you include prewritten questions on the slide, always configure the presentation software to present only one at a time. If you present several questions at once, participants may feel lost or skip a question in favor of one they believe is more important.

Depending on the audience, prewritten questions have the potential to stifle discussion. After hearing an acceptable answer, participants may feel compelled to wait for the next question instead of bringing forward a question or concern. Given this possibility, it may be ideal for the facilitator to avoid displaying prewritten questions on the screen and instead ask them verbally. The prewritten questions can be saved in the presentation software's notes section, displayed on the side of the presenting computer's screen.

We'll revisit prewritten questions and how to use them during an exercise in Chapter 4.

The Debrief

During this final phase, dedicate a slide or two to a debrief. This can be an open-ended discussion or a series of prewritten questions. Either way, you should review the people, processes, and technologies in place and whether the organization has the resources to handle an incident like the one rehearsed during the exercise. Chapter 5 will provide more guidance on how to most effectively perform a debrief after a tabletop exercise.

NOTE   *See the appendix for several example deliverables you could use in a tabletop exercise. We highly recommend modifying these to fit your organization's needs rather than using them as is.*

Inviting Feedback

Now that you're approaching the finish line of your tabletop exercise development, consider soliciting feedback from organizational or industry peers, such as those who weighed in on the scenario design process. They could offer avenues of exploration you hadn't considered, enriching the exercise.

Keep in mind that if you share any organizational information with an outside party, whether it be policy documents or a PowerPoint deck, you need to adhere to the company's information disclosure processes. Seek approval in writing from appropriate stakeholders before sending information to outside parties. For some organizations, sharing information externally is never acceptable; for others, sitting down with an industry peer over lunch and sharing your plan is perfectly acceptable with permission.

Summary

Once you complete the steps described in this chapter, you should have the materials you'll need to deliver the tabletop exercise. This means the development team has agreed on a relevant and realistic scenario and broken it into logical components via injects.

The next chapter discusses facilitation strategies to employ during the actual event. You're almost there!

Questions

In the development process, the rubber meets the road, as you'll formulate ideas and narrow them down until you've drafted your scenario. When embarking on this process, answer the following questions before moving into the next phase:

1. What is your process for selecting a topic? Once you have a list of potential topics, how will you narrow it down to your final choice? Likewise, what is the process for selecting a final scenario?

2. Is the final scenario realistic, relevant to the organization and to participants, and developed to account for known or potential weaknesses?

3. Are any injects focused on a particular function, such as legal?

4. Do the injects have the desired and appropriate escalation pace?

5. How do you intend to encourage participation in the tabletop exercise?

6. Will an educational briefing prior to the tabletop exercise be valuable to the participants?

7. Who in the organization might be able to review the storyboard and provide critical feedback? Could you ask industry peers to review the tabletop exercise materials?

4

FACILITATING A SUCCESSFUL TABLETOP EXERCISE

Now that the preparation work is complete, it's time to deliver the tabletop exercise. This chapter puts you in the role of facilitator and covers a number of strategies that will help ensure your event is productive. Some of these are guidelines you can follow to stay organized and balance your responsibilities as facilitator, and others are recommendations for tools and techniques to boost participant engagement and create a more interactive exercise.

The Facilitator's Role

If you're facilitating the tabletop, you have the challenging role of guiding participants through the scenario while simultaneously encouraging discussion. Even for seasoned facilitators, this can be a demanding task at times. Although each tabletop is different, you should limit yourself to the following tasks:

- Providing clarification, when needed, about the scenario and injects
- Controlling the discussion so that the group can explore topics in their entirety while ensuring they don't waste time going down rabbit holes that don't align with the exercise's objectives
- Identifying comments and concerns that warrant additional discussion
- Injecting your own professional expertise by asking targeted questions to explore potential deficiencies
- Recording themes and potential deficiencies to document after the tabletop exercise
- Keeping track of timing and working through the scenario at the appropriate pace

A facilitator is akin to a referee at a sporting event; you should allow the participants to discuss the scenario and intervene only when necessary.

This means, first, that you must avoid dominating the conversation. As a rule of thumb, you should aim to speak no more than 30 percent of the time. Some facilitators mistakenly think they must control all aspects of the conversation; unfortunately, this discourages collaboration between attendees and fosters an environment where issues are less likely to emerge.

You should also avoid "leading the witness" by overly managing the discussion. While attendees might sometimes need to be nudged in a particular direction, it is far more effective for you to ask questions that enable attendees to explore the topic on their own. This process fosters a more robust dialogue.

Don't be afraid to tactfully challenge attendees by pushing back on an answer's validity. Consider the following example:

> **Facilitator:** How would you know how long the threat actor had access to the system?
>
> **Network administrator:** We would know this after looking at the logs. The logs should go back 60 days.
>
> **Facilitator:** Is the log retention period documented anywhere?
>
> **Network administrator:** It isn't. This is a normal time for us to retain logs based on size. Once the logs hit a certain size, they overwrite themselves.
>
> **Facilitator:** What happens if the server is very active?
>
> **Network administrator:** The logs might be there for only a few days.

In this interaction, the facilitator's follow-up questions surfaced two important issues: (1) there was no documented log retention standard, and (2) with the current log retention scheme and a very active server, it's possible that only a few days' worth of logs would be available. If the facilitator hadn't followed up on the network administrator's initial answer, the exercise would have missed these important findings. However, you should avoid challenging every statement even if you are highly skilled in certain topics—you don't want to create an adversarial environment or come across as a know-it-all.

Finally, you must always conduct yourself in a respectful and professional manner, even when an attendee says something that borders on outright incompetence (and may be recognized as such by other participants). In these situations, you must respond in a way that doesn't belittle or embarrass them but still makes them aware of their error.

Tabletop Management Tasks

The facilitation process can be incredibly mentally taxing. You must simultaneously process attendee input and questions, scan the group for visual cues, keep the focus on the scenario, ensure that key points get addressed, maintain a tactful and attentive dialogue, defer to positions of authority in the room, and note any process deficiencies to be addressed in a follow-up report.

Needless to say, this role can challenge even the most organized individuals. The facilitation management tasks discussed in this section can help you reduce fatigue and focus on the discussion.

Assigning a Scribe

One of the simplest methods of reducing your burden as facilitator is to completely eliminate one of your tasks: tracking the issues, deficiencies, and recommendations that will eventually find their way into the post-tabletop report. You can assign these tasks to what is commonly referred to as a *scribe*. This person doesn't need to be an expert in information security or a related field; they just need to be familiar with the scenario so they can understand the exercise's context, goals, objectives, and the role of the participants.

The role of the scribe can easily be filled by a junior employee who might have a lighter schedule than most employees and could use the experience to learn about organizational dynamics and cybersecurity. Alternatively, the scribe could be someone in a mid-level function with a vested interest in the tabletop exercise's outcome. For example, a risk management professional would likely benefit from viewing the incident response process and understanding the issues that emerge.

The scribe must coordinate with you before the tabletop exercise to understand in advance what to track. While you're facilitating the event, you should also have a discreet way of signaling (a glance or other nonverbal gesture, for example) when the scribe should record an important point.

In addition to taking notes, the scribe could create an initial draft of the report for you to review. We discuss reporting in Chapter 5.

Adding a Co-facilitator

Another way to ease the burden of facilitation is to recruit a co-facilitator. This person can take on tasks like scanning the audience for questions or managing the presentation software. By agreeing to divide and conquer tasks in advance, you'll each have fewer responsibilities. Also, one of you can take mental breaks while the other addresses a line of questioning. This gives you both opportunities to briefly reflect on the status of the tabletop exercise, contemplate future lines of questioning, and take a moment to mentally recharge.

However, it's important to choose a compatible co-facilitator. Compatibility comes in many forms, including:

Personality   Co-facilitating a tabletop requires close collaboration during all phases of the exercise. Choose someone with whom you can enjoy a cup of coffee (and not someone with whom you find yourself constantly checking your phone for an excuse to depart). You don't need to be best friends; however, facilitators should have a degree of workplace chemistry.

Coordination   Ensure that you're able to coordinate in real time while in front of an audience. This helps ensure that transitions between you during the exercise are as natural and seamless as possible.

Facilitation styles   Some facilitators have an aggressive delivery style, while others are more passive. Avoid mixing facilitator styles, which could give attendees whiplash as they adjust between questions from each facilitator. A tabletop exercise shouldn't make the attendees feel like they're in a game of good cop/bad cop.

In addition, having a co-facilitator can bring in different viewpoints and subject matter expertise. While one of you may be an expert in risk management, the other might be skilled in network security. These complementary skill sets could add more value to the exercise.

Inviting a Guest Presenter

To break up your facilitator role, you could invite a guest presenter to introduce specific facts in an inject. For example, if an inject for a senior-level tabletop communicates a new set of facts from the IT security team (such as the confirmed loss of sensitive data), the actual IT security manager could enter the room to brief the attendees.

A guest presenter should present facts just as they would in a real incident. For example, the IT security manager could use the opportunity to practice announcing newly confirmed technical information. In addition to making the tabletop exercise more interactive, using a guest presenter has the benefit of acquainting participants with someone who would be involved in the response to a real information security incident. However, be sure to brief the guest presenter on anything they shouldn't say to keep them from spoiling unknowns or contradicting scenario details.

Prewriting Questions

A common facilitation technique is to enter the event with several questions ready to ask participants. This is yet another way that you can better manage the litany of facilitation tasks during the exercise.

In some tabletop exercises, attendees participate readily, and you might have trouble keeping track of the many valuable points they bring up. Having questions readily available for each inject can save you from trying to remember whether a fruitful discussion addressed all the important points. Alternatively, the audience may give short answers and engage minimally, leaving you struggling to find ways to spark the conversation. During such situations, having prewritten questions can help you jump-start stalled discussions.

Prewritten questions could be tied to a particular inject, or they could be generic and asked at any time. Make sure, however, that they align with the goals of the exercise and are appropriate for the participants. For example, if you aim to determine whether the organization has the proper tooling to detect and contain a cybersecurity incident, your questions probably shouldn't focus on how to notify and update executive leadership of a breach.

You should understand the correct answers to the questions you ask, ideally based on formal documentation. For example, if one of your questions involves log retention, you should be aware of a company policy requiring that select logs be maintained for 90 days. The point of asking questions you already know the answer to isn't to pounce on a wrong answer; rather, it's to help you craft pertinent follow-up questions and enhance your knowledge of the topic.

You might want to work with the trusted agent on this task, as they'll likely understand the questions worth asking as well as their correct answers. Examples of prewritten questions include:

- Given what you know, what tools or logs do you have to confirm the known facts?
- Based on the information provided, is this a cybersecurity incident?
- With this new information, do additional stakeholders need to be notified?
- Given the current known facts of the incident, who is in charge of the response?

For each of these questions, there should be documentation that provides the correct answer (or at least superficial guidance).

Finally, prewritten questions are an effective crutch if you feel nervous at the prospect of facilitating a tabletop exercise. While managing the numerous other exercise management tasks, you may find yourself stuck during a lull in conversation; having a question ready to go can be a godsend in that situation.

Exercise Tools and Tactics

There are a variety of tools at your disposal to assist with the tabletop exercise, ranging from a simple whiteboard and easel to live, online polling software. Of course, the fact that a new shiny tool exists doesn't mean that it would be appropriate for the audience or enhance the exercise—or that you'll know how to use it. You must be skilled at using any aids you bring along. A live tabletop exercise is not the time to troubleshoot a new technology or determine that you haven't enabled the correct setting (and doing so is a surefire way to earn a collective facepalm from your audience).

NOTE *Some of the suggestions in this section involve using technology to assist you in facilitating the exercise. Prior to doing so, make sure the technology is allowed. For example, does policy or business practice permit you to load certain software or store tabletop data on a company laptop or tablet? Some highly regulated environments prohibit the use of tools like remote presentation platforms, so it's essential to understand any constraints in advance.*

A Writing Board

You or your scribe could use a writing board (such as a whiteboard, paper flipchart, or chalkboard) to record points as they emerge. This is particularly helpful when participants repeat an issue in a discussion; you can politely point to the writing board and remind them that it has already been discussed and recorded.

A writing board can also serve as a "parking lot" for questions or concerns that need to be explored. Attendees sometimes fire off a battery of questions, and writing those items on the board "parks" them until you're ready to explore them. This keeps you in control of the discussion's flow while assuring attendees that their issue won't be forgotten.

If no writing board is available in the conference room, you could purchase an easel and flipchart to bring to the event. As previously discussed, make sure you're aware of the features and shortcomings of the room before the time of your exercise.

Polling Software

One strategy to increase participation in a tabletop exercise you're facilitating is to add interactive elements. For example, using polling software can be an excellent way to elicit audience interaction. Polling software lets you present a question to participants, who can answer using a smartphone, tablet, or laptop. As the participants answer, the responses might appear in real time, after a predetermined period, or when you end the submission period.

Polling software does require some additional coordination, and most polling software platforms have a nominal fee; however, they're easy to use. Some online presentation platforms have built-in polling capabilities, eliminating the need for an add-on service.

Consider the following examples where polling software may be helpful:

- During an exercise intended to assess whether attendees are following the correct process, you could display a poll question asking whether a certain set of conditions would require notifying information security personnel. This could demonstrate whether attendees are taking the appropriate actions.

- By providing a question with a free-form answer, you could verify whether attendees respond with different and conflicting responses. This would demonstrate a lack of alignment on processes and the need for education.

- Recording poll questions during a tabletop exercise may help satisfy an audit requirement and function as evidence of participation.

A simple way to use polling software is to ask a question after presenting a set of facts. For example, Figure 4-1 shows a poll question for an inject that asks, "Based on the known facts, would the following scenario be considered a cybersecurity incident?" The audience can visit the given URL to submit their answers.

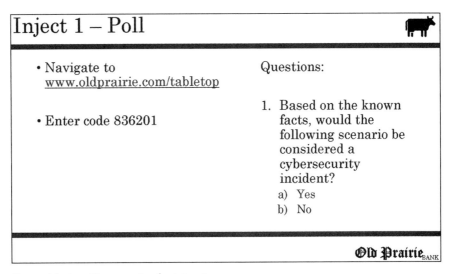

Figure 4-1: A polling question for Inject 1

Figure 4-2 shows the results automatically populated in the presentation deck, either in real time or when the facilitator chooses. The results help the facilitator explore whether the audience's answers align with the organization's policy and if there are reasons for the deviation.

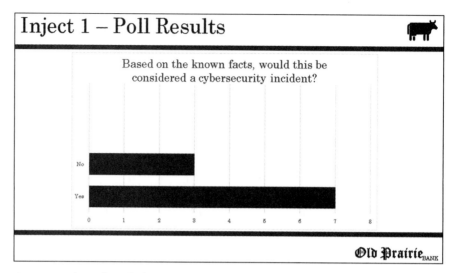

Figure 4-2: The poll results for the Inject 1 poll

Polling software also provides the opportunity to ask questions that require more than a yes or no answer. For example, if you're exploring who participants believe has the authority to take certain containment actions, such as shutting down key network segments or disconnecting the internet, forcing them to fill in an answer box on a survey may provide interesting results. As you can see in Figure 4-3, responses to a poll question mostly coalesced around two names (Jennifer and Taylor) but included a few others. Such a result may indicate that the organization needs to better define who is authorized to take specific, potentially drastic actions.

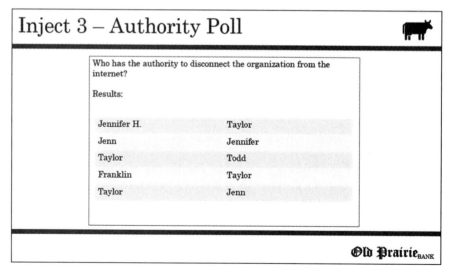

Figure 4-3: Results of an open-ended poll

Another benefit of using polling software is that it lets you automatically capture data points that you can use for reporting. Automatically recording these answers saves time and can provide details that support your recommendations.

As helpful as they can be, don't use polls arbitrarily; they should always be oriented toward a particular issue.

Also bear in mind that technology is a fickle mistress. The actual tabletop exercise is not the time to discover that you need to adjust a default configuration. Rehearse using the polling software just as you will during the tabletop exercise.

Remote Presentation Software

If facilitating the tabletop exercise remotely, you must understand how to operate each feature of your remote presentation software. This is especially important if you're external to the organization but required to use its tools. Fumbling with the software is a good way to lose credibility and frustrate those who devoted time to the event.

Features of remote presentation software vary greatly but probably include:

- The ability to create breakout rooms, which isolate groups of participants in their own virtual rooms to collaborate on a particular topic and then reconvene in the larger room
- Question and answer management, such as features that let attendees "raise their hands" when they wish to ask a question
- Onscreen whiteboards that facilitators can use to record issues and recommendations
- The ability to spotlight a singular person, such as the facilitator, so camera views won't constantly shift to whoever is speaking

Just as with the polling software, you should thoroughly test all features with multiple peers.

It's also important to establish ground rules for collaborating virtually at the onset of the tabletop exercise. Attendees may not be aware of certain features, so they might benefit from a quick primer on how to use those options. Common ground rules include:

- Requiring attendees to "raise their hand" and be acknowledged before asking questions. This keeps multiple people from attempting to speak at the same time.
- Mandating that all attendees turn their camera on so they can't hide or focus on other tasks such as email. Note that this mandate may not align with the organization's culture, so you should confirm it with the organization in advance if you are an outside facilitator. Also, avoid "camera shaming"—we've all had days where the last thing we want to do is be on camera in front of our peers.

- Encouraging attendees to mute themselves when not speaking to eliminate unwanted and distracting background noise.

- Creating a framework for using the chat room to ask questions, provide additional feedback, or accomplish some other purpose.

Convey these ground rules to participants in advance to ensure they have ample time to prepare. In today's age of remote working, not everyone works at a desk with a properly mounted camera and quality microphone. Communicating requirements early enables participants to plan a suitable location and participate in a professional manner.

A co-facilitator or scribe can take on the role of monitoring the chat room, watching for raised hands, and maintaining a whiteboard. Especially during a hybrid tabletop exercise, using these features can be mentally taxing, as you have to pay attention both to a roomful of tabletop attendees and to those communicating remotely.

Multimedia Aids

Multimedia aids, such as short video or audio clips, can help captivate your audience and break up the monotony of a slideshow. However, these tools must be relevant to the information presented thus far in the exercise. Attendees shouldn't be left wondering how a video connects to the scenario. Consider the following examples of relevant multimedia aids:

- During a scenario involving ransomware, play an audio file found on a server impacted by ransomware. The audio file can contain an ominous voice (the threat actor's) making it clear that the ransom must be paid within 48 hours or all data will be destroyed. Having a voice to connect with the threat actor adds a degree of realism.

- In a tabletop exercise for a hospital's executive staff, greet attendees with a video of a news anchor informing the audience of a large breach at the hospital, complete with examples of data lost, panoramic shots of the hospital's exterior, and an interview with a disgruntled patient, angry that their personal data was lost.

Implementing these examples will take additional time and resources. However, they will help avoid the tedium of a long presentation deck, look professional, and create a better experience.

CASE STUDY: "NO COMMENT"

Willow Creek Northern Electric Cooperative was reeling after a series of high-profile power outages caused by improper maintenance. The outages were particularly impactful, as they had forced a 911 emergency call center to go offline, as well as a hospital and nursing home to lose power. While the call center and hospital had backup systems, the backup generators had failed at

---

the nursing home, and elderly patients had been left in sweltering heat, according to news reports. The media had also camped outside Willow Creek's headquarters to interview its staff, which resulted in embarrassing sound bites on the evening news.

Willow Creek acknowledged that it hadn't trained its staff on responding to media inquiries. Over the next six months, its media relations team promoted the policy that staff should direct all inquiries to the proper channels; if confronted directly, they should politely state "no comment" and walk away.

Later that year, Willow Creek began planning a ransomware-focused operational-level tabletop exercise. When providing feedback to the development team, the executive sponsor brought up the ugly sound bites still circulating on the internet and asked that the exercise weave in the media relations education employees had recently received.

The development team had an idea. The IT director, who had a family member in the local university's media department, arranged to have a camera operator and reporter outside the building during the exercise. During a break, the facilitator told the attendees that a food truck was parked outside. Two attendees at a time could head to the truck to keep from overwhelming the truck's small staff.

After each pair of attendees placed their order at the food truck, the reporter and camera operator emerged, firing off a series of questions while pointing a microphone in the hungry attendees' faces. "Can you comment on the ransomware outbreak? Will it impact power? Is this the nursing home fiasco all over again? The community is scared!"

At the end of the exercise (and much to the audience's dismay), the reporter and camera operator entered the room to share a few video clips. A few of the participants had responded "no comment," as the media training had urged, but several had provided meandering answers, and at least one had answered in a way that was outright problematic. (The development team left this single problematic answer out of the public debrief to avoid embarrassment.)

While it took additional effort, the activity effectively tested the success of the media training, proving the training hadn't thoroughly mitigated the risk of employees speaking to the news. The findings were likely valid, as the exercise had simulated a stressful, real-world media encounter. Now attendees couldn't merely say, "I wouldn't talk to the media, because I was trained on the proper procedures." The activity also broke up the monotony of a traditional PowerPoint-based presentation.

Attendee Tasks and Breakout Groups

While not appropriate for all tabletop exercises due to logistical constraints, assigning a task to a specific function could add dynamism to the event. For example, if an employee in charge of media relations states they would issue a press release within 15 minutes of an event occurring, you could request that they move to a side room to craft the statement. Assigning a task during a tabletop is also easy to implement during a remote exercise, as most remote presentation tools have a breakout feature; with a few clicks of the mouse, you can place certain attendees in an isolated meeting for a set duration.

However, you must be careful to ensure that this action won't embarrass attendees if they're unprepared to perform the requested task. You don't want to inhibit the fostering of relationships.

Recording Devices and Software

Some facilitators might wonder if they should record the tabletop exercise. Recording has become easier in the post–COVID-19 world, where it's more likely that the exercise will use remote collaboration software that lets you record meetings and save them to a sharable file with the click of a button.

More often than not, however, recording has negative consequences. It tends to have a chilling effect on tabletop exercises, mitigating their effectiveness. Successful tabletop exercises are contingent on honest, open, and frank dialogue, and participants are less likely to contribute if they fear being recorded giving incorrect answers or going against the grain of organizational norms.

While there may be legitimate reasons for recording a tabletop exercise (for example, if a scribe is unavailable and you'd like to revisit the responses for the eventual report), it generally isn't recommended unless a clear benefit outweighs the potential negative effects.

Making the Most of the Exercise Space

Over time, each facilitator learns techniques they can use during a tabletop exercise to set them up for success. Some of these techniques involve planning how you'll use the space, such as determining the best conference room seating arrangement and how you'll communicate with team members.

Maximize the Conference Room Layout

An often-neglected facilitation technique is to use the environment to foster dialogue. If a conference room's tables all face the front, the attendees will direct their attention toward you as the facilitator. This could be counterproductive, making attendees less likely to engage with one another.

A better layout would be to arrange the tables in a U-shape (option 1 in Figure 4-4). In this arrangement, the attendees can face one another, observe one another's body language, and direct comments toward particular attendees while making eye contact. It also enables you to easily walk into the U-shape and maintain close proximity with all attendees throughout the discussion.

Some conference rooms consist of a large round or rectangular table that can't be split up. In these situations, it's generally a good idea to stand opposite the displayed presentation (option 2 in Figure 4-4) so that attendees can split their attention between the front of the room (where the presentation is displayed) and the back (where you are), ensuring that there isn't a single focal point. This type of setup also encourages more interaction among attendees.

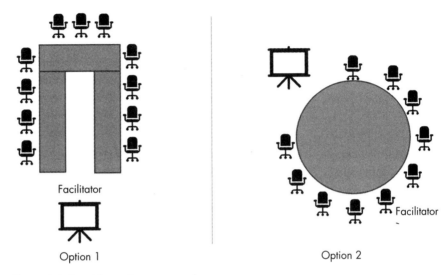

Figure 4-4: Possible conference room layouts

Of course, there are various other possible room configurations. Prior to the presentation, think about which one will best encourage dialogue. Also, when selecting a location for the tabletop exercise, make sure you're able to move the tables into an ideal layout. Booking a conference room only to find out that you're stuck with its undesirable table layout is never a great way to start an exercise.

Work the Room to Boost Engagement

The most engaging speakers move around the room. Politely walking up to an attendee to ask them a question is a far more personable strategy than speaking to them from the front of the room. Doing so also offers the opportunity to direct a question to a certain person.

Sometimes the facilitator can inadvertently impair a perfectly productive conversation by sending unintended cues to the audience. For example, directly looking at an attendee while they make a comment to another attendee may make them think you want them to wrap up their point. In these cases, take a few steps back away from the attendees to physically remove yourself from the conversation until it has run its course.

Avoid standing at a lectern. Although lecterns provide cables, a microphone, a place to put a laptop, and a surface to quickly jot down notes, they may inhibit participant engagement by placing a physical barrier between you and the audience. Wireless presentation remotes enable you to advance slides and perform basic presentation tasks without having to continually return to a lectern. If you expect attendees to connect remotely, however, investigate the room's audiovisual equipment, as certain systems may force you to stay near the single speakerphone.

Communication Tips

This section outlines some of the many communication strategies you could use to conduct a high-quality tabletop exercise. Some may seem like common sense; however, in the moment, it's easy to forget the simple principles that make an event successful.

Monitor Physiological Responses

For some facilitators, tabletop exercises can be highly stressful and increase breathing rate, talking speed, and perspiration. These physiological responses could distract attendees, so you should attempt to mitigate them. Prior to the exercise, take stock of any physiological responses you commonly experience when presenting and make a plan to address them should they appear. If you're feeling especially nervous, there are a number of simple methods you could employ:

• If you're at a logical breaking point, announce a five-minute break for attendees to refresh drinks, visit the bathroom, or tend to email.

• Ask the co-facilitator to take on the next inject.

• Try to consciously regulate your breathing.

• Ask an attendee a question to foster a short dialogue between two participants and shift focus away from you.

Everyone reacts to stressful situations in different ways. As the facilitator, it's important for you to be aware of potential reactions and be able to initiate effective mitigation strategies on the fly if needed.

Set Up Backchannels

Before the tabletop exercise, it can be helpful to set up a backchannel for communications with your trusted agent or executive sponsor so you can convey key information to each other outside the audience's watchful eyes.

Backchannels are usually best reserved for remotely facilitated tabletop exercises, where they can consist of a side chat room. During an in-person exercise, a backchannel is more difficult to implement but not impossible; the trusted agent can send you a short message on a strategically positioned cell phone. However, you must be careful not to let that distract you from your other facilitation tasks or make it obvious that you are communicating with someone else in the room, which could be awkward in some situations.

Backchannels are often used to give the facilitator a nudge to explore a subject. For example, if you're discussing data backup methodologies and haven't yet discussed whether the backups are tested (a common business continuity/disaster recovery failure), the trusted agent can request that the topic be addressed. Alternatively, the backchannel could provide an opportunity to connect with an executive sponsor, ask them how the exercise is going, and make adjustments as necessary.

Backchannels are especially important for external consultants acting as facilitators. Lacking institutional knowledge, they could easily miss a key issue that a trusted agent would recognize. But for some facilitators, the extra mental task could detract from their ability to conduct a quality exercise.

Check in with Senior Attendees

Attendees at a tabletop exercise represent a range of seniority. During a break, it's prudent to check in privately with the most senior attendee to ensure that the exercise aligns with their expectations. This check-in may be as simple as saying, "I just wanted to make sure this is meeting your expectations. Is there anything we should explore further or be sure to address?" This gives the senior member an opportunity to voice any concerns or get reassurance that an issue will be addressed in a future inject. Also check in with the executive sponsor if they're attending the tabletop exercise.

Checking in allows you to course-correct if needed and mitigates the risk that the senior member will complain about the event later. (If they do, you can politely note that they had previously provided positive feedback.) This is especially helpful if you're external to the company, as external vendors are more likely to receive criticism.

Manage Conversation Hogs

It's not uncommon for one attendee to dominate the conversation, effectively shutting down others and harming the exercise. This person most likely isn't trying to grandstand. Instead, their behavior is probably due to a combination of factors, including the following:

- A desire to demonstrate that they have answers to every problem
- A lack of social skills
- The fact that the organization's existing processes place all responsibilities during a cybersecurity incident on one person
- The organization's culture of deferring to one person

As facilitator, you could also inadvertently encourage their behavior by failing to ask questions targeting the other attendees. There are many different strategies for mitigating the conversation monopolizer, including these:

- Jokingly point out that although they have all the answers, it would be great to hear from others. Then ask a question of another attendee that doesn't relate to the dominating employee's skill set.
- During a break, privately but politely ask them to let other attendees carry the baton. You can frame this in a way that takes the employee's feelings into account. For example, you could say, "You clearly know

what to do during an incident. I would love it if we could give others a chance to step up to the plate."

- Artificially remove them from the scenario by adding information that would make them unreachable. For example, announce that they're now on a plane heading to meet a vendor and unable to communicate for the next two injects. Alternatively, display an image of a scuba diver, then inform them that they are now on vacation. If they tell you they're never without their cell phone, you can respond, "You're scuba diving off the Galápagos Islands; your cell phone is very wet and doesn't work."

Whatever strategy you use, you should handle the situation with respect and tact. Pointing out that an individual's behavior is borderline rude is a surefire way to alienate them, as well as other attendees.

Forge Interpersonal Connections

Successful tabletop facilitators are able to forge interpersonal connections and make attendees feel at ease before the first inject even appears. Bonding with attendees is a challenge. Most relationships are forged over shared experiences; unfortunately, you may have only 15 minutes as attendees enter the room to develop a personal connection. For better or worse, the attention you give them during these important 15 minutes may make or break the exercise's success. Every facilitator has their own strategy for bonding with participants. Consider these options:

- Talk about the weather. It may sound boring, but it's one of the most universal topics, whether it be a heat spell last month or an upcoming snowstorm.

- Discuss sports. More than likely, some of the participants follow sports. Commenting on last night's win, a miserable season, or a sports team logo on a participant's lanyard is an effective way to engage them.

- Bring up local culture. This may include regional activities, such as hiking at a nearby mountain or local cuisine. Asking the audience of a tabletop in Baltimore who serves the best crab cakes in town, for example, will likely generate passionate opinions.

- Share details about your family. Families, relationships, and parenting are universal topics in almost any audience. Bringing up a funny story about your children or a parent's quirkiness will almost always prompt others to share similar stories.

- Discuss shared job issues. When meeting someone working in a certain role, discuss a topic that impacts both of your jobs. For example, a finance professional may be just as concerned about the fast-moving cyber insurance market as you are.

- Mention cybersecurity news. The latest cybersecurity headline or zero-day exploit makes for an easy topic of interest.

A brief, friendly conversation with a participant puts them at ease and makes them more likely to participate in the exercise.

Do not discuss potentially controversial topics, such as the current state of management at the organization, politics, foreign policy, or religion. These potentially polarizing topics are minefields that can easily offend an attendee and start the exercise on the wrong note.

Consider the Question Structure

One of the facilitator's goals is to encourage dialogue. To do so, you must be cognizant of how you structure the questions you ask attendees. Questions that require short or yes or no answers are less likely to generate discussion. Consider the following three questions that commonly emerge in a cybersecurity tabletop exercise and how you could reformat them to generate greater audience interaction:

Question 1

- **Original format:** Is it acceptable to shut down the local network?
- **Modified format:** What conditions need to occur for it to be acceptable to shut down the local network?

The original format could elicit a yes or no answer from the audience, which would yield less discussion fodder. The modified question assumes that it is at some point acceptable to shut down the local network; to respond, participants must contemplate the conditions that play into such a decision.

Question 2

- **Original format:** Is this personally identifiable information?
- **Modified format:** What is personally identifiable information? Is this it?

The modified format asks a compound question to foster a discussion about what qualifies as personally identifiable information.

Question 3

- **Original format:** Does the CISO need to know?
- **Modified format:** What needs to happen for the CISO to be informed? And do they need to be woken up in the middle of the night?

In the original format, the attendees would all likely nod if the injects conveyed a set of facts that were severe enough to necessitate notifying a CISO. In the modified format, the attendees need to contemplate what conditions must exist to notify the CISO and, depending on the urgency, if those conditions are bad enough to wake a senior employee in the middle of the night.

Questions can also artificially create a discussion between two attendees. For example, if you want two employees, such as team members from information technology (Bob) and human resources (Luz), to engage with each other, you might ask, "Bob, if during the incident you discovered that an employee was using their personal email to exchange sensitive company information, which is clearly against policy, would you confront that employee? Luz, as the human resources focal, what is your role here? Is there a defined process? Would you want to be present when the employee is confronted?"

There is certainly a time and place for questions that generate short answers. However, well-structured questions can create a more interactive tabletop exercise.

Pay Attention to Nonverbal Communication

In their book *Nonverbal Communication* (Routledge, 2022), Burgoon, Manusov, and Guerrero state that "nonverbal cues pervade virtually every communicative act." Nonverbal communication can include facial expressions, eye contact, proximity, posture, and other silent signals.

Give significant thought to your nonverbal communication, whether it's maintaining eye contact with an individual or a group of attendees when asking a question, using a caring tone when pointing out a significant process deficiency, or smiling to convey a welcoming demeanor. Consider these examples of nonverbal communication and how each may promote discussion during a tabletop exercise:

- You might notice that a member of the organization's communications team has been largely disengaged. You don't want to publicly call them out, so instead you ask the group a question but specifically make eye contact and give a friendly smile to the disengaged attendee.

- A member of the information security team makes a particularly salient point that you believe will end up as a key recommendation. You very intentionally lean forward in your seat, furrow your eyebrows, and make eye contact with the information security team member to convey that you're interested in the point. Without a word, you've indicated the point's importance to the other attendees.

- An attendee expresses frustration about an identified process shortcoming. You place your palm on your face and groan slightly. The employee, recognizing that you understand their pain, continues to provide information.

Seasoned facilitators use several of these nonverbal communication tactics to better engage the audience and deliver a more effective tabletop exercise.

Practice Cultural Awareness

In a globalized workforce, you might be conducting a tabletop exercise with participants scattered across the globe. A company's development team may be in Australia, its manufacturing operations in Kenya, and its e-commerce team in Vietnam. Each team follows different cultural norms that could impact the tabletop exercise. If you aren't aware of these norms, you could make an offensive remark that may alienate an attendee or, worse, elicit an angry response. Examples of cultural norm violations may include:

- Not showing the proper deference to the attendee hierarchy and failing to introduce the most senior member first.
- Criticizing a response from an attendee in an environment where criticism is rare, which might embarrass them in front of their peers.
- Making statements about a government or political philosophy that could be seen as attacking a culture.
- Not being aware of conflicts based on nationalism or religion and seeming out of touch.

Prior to the tabletop exercise, take stock of where each attendee is physically located and research basic business and cultural norms. In general, if you're unsure whether a statement may be seen as insensitive, avoid the topic.

Identify Sensitive Topics Beforehand

In every organization, certain events or topics are sensitive to bring up in conversation. Identifying them is especially important for external consultants, who might not be aware of the relevant context. Examples of such minefields include the following:

- Discussing shortcomings in the security operation center case management system when everyone is already aware (and frustrated) that this system has been a complete and continual failure.
- Bringing up the process used to terminate employees during a conversation about insider threats when the organization recently experienced a surprise layoff.

Prior to the tabletop exercise, ask the executive sponsor or other points of contact about topics to avoid. Keep in mind that there is a difference between asking tough questions and asking questions that betray a lack of awareness or sensitivity. When in doubt, however, consider avoiding a certain discussion point.

Summary

Facilitating a tabletop exercise is much more than simply firing up a presentation and hoping for the best. Successful tabletop exercise facilitators use a range of tools and techniques, as discussed in this chapter, to craft an effective session.

After facilitating a successful exercise, you might feel like you've crossed the finish line, but there are many follow-up steps to complete. These steps, discussed in the next chapter, are the most important aspects of the tabletop as they codify findings and equip the organization to make improvements after the event.

Questions

Consider the following questions ahead of the facilitation process to make the event go smoothly and remove some of your burden as facilitator:

1. Who will take notes during the exercise? Is it possible to assign a dedicated scribe? What are the scribe's specific tasks?
2. Will you ask prewritten questions?
3. Will you use any facilitation aids, such as a whiteboard, polling software, or an easel? If the exercise is in person, what aids does the facility already have in place, and what will you need to procure prior to the exercise? If the exercise is remote, what tools will you leverage?
4. Although doing so isn't generally recommended, will you record the tabletop exercise? If so, do the benefits of recording outweigh its impact on attendees?
5. Should you set up a communication backchannel with certain attendees, such as the executive sponsor? How will you communicate with them to avoid distracting attendees or neglecting other facilitation tasks?
6. How will the conference room be laid out? Can you make changes to it prior to the exercise?
7. If you're nervous about presenting, what techniques will you use to control your physiological responses (such as speaking too fast)?
8. Does the development team anticipate that any attendees will dominate the discussion? What strategies can you use to mitigate this?
9. What strategies can you use to bond with attendees prior to the tabletop exercise? Have you built in time for a meet and greet?
10. Are there unique cultural nuances to be aware of?

5

ACTING ON WHAT YOU'VE LEARNED: EVALUATION AND NEXT STEPS

The most important work occurs after the conclusion of the exercise, in the evaluation phase. In this stage, you will identify and record any issues the organization should remedy. Without this follow-up, a tabletop exercise may be far less valuable.

Once the tabletop exercise concludes, you'll need a plan to gather feedback, craft a report, and determine the next steps for the organization. This chapter will walk you through that process and various points to consider as you perform these activities.

Evaluation Requirements and Restrictions

Before planning specific evaluation activities, the development team should take stock of any requirements or restrictions. Evaluation *requirements* could come from external regulatory bodies (such as a state insurance commission) or be contractual (such as an agreement with a vendor or outside party). An organization's cyber insurance carrier, for example, may state that in order to maintain coverage or see a favorable premium, the organization must conduct a tabletop exercise on an annual basis and document it with a report containing the scenario outline, attendees, and key recommendations. Alternatively, the organization's risk management team may require that the development team create a report with identified recommendations, named stakeholders, and parties responsible for addressing any shortcomings.

The development team also needs to be aware of any legal *restrictions* imposed on the evaluation process. For example, the legal team may express reservations about putting certain information in writing. If sensitive data were stolen during a cybersecurity incident and there was a written document citing a high likelihood of this data being stolen, it could create a legal risk. For this reason (among others), the development team should confer with the organization's legal resources to understand any requirements or restrictions prior to creating any documentation.

Choosing an Evaluator

Prior to the tabletop exercise, the development team should choose someone to oversee the evaluation phase and identify the recommendations to include in the report. This evaluator should understand a variety of organizational functions, as the event will likely reveal shortcomings that span multiple roles. For example, Table 5-1 lists potential issues that a single cybersecurity tabletop exercise could uncover, as well as the teams that would most likely be responsible for addressing them.

Table 5-1: Identified Issues and Responding Teams

Issue	Responding team
A lack of understanding of compliance obligations during a ransomware incident	Finance, legal
A recognition that an attacker could take advantage of lax security procedures at several facilities	Physical security, risk management
An unclear process for how the organization would communicate with customers and vendors regarding a public-facing cybersecurity incident	Communications, legal

In many tabletop exercises, a member of the development team, such as the development lead or facilitator, functions as the evaluator.

 This chapter assumes that the facilitator is also functioning as the evaluator, as this is most often the case.

In organizations with resources to bear, a member of the risk management or audit team can take on this role. Risk management, which is normally tasked with identifying and addressing risks across the organization, is a logical choice for the evaluation, as each finding is a risk that could impact the company's ability to respond to a cybersecurity incident. Audit would be another logical choice: some of the findings may highlight deviations from policies (or the lack of an established policy) that need to be addressed.

Unfortunately, organizations with constrained resources might not be able to include additional personnel or might lack risk management and audit roles.

Evaluation Methods

This section describes several common methods of evaluation. Each organization has its own goals and objectives, however, so be sure to account for those when determining which methods to use.

Ideally, the evaluator should present a road map of these activities at the beginning of the tabletop exercise so attendees can understand how their comments will be used and what the overall evaluation process will be.

Performing a Debrief

Immediately after concluding the tabletop exercise, the evaluator should conduct a two-stage debrief: first, gathering feedback from attendees, and second, gathering feedback from select stakeholders, such as the executive sponsor or the most senior participants. While the evaluator will request additional feedback from attendees later, soliciting feedback right at the conclusion of the exercise gets people's thoughts when the exercise is still fresh in their minds.

For the first stage of the debrief, allot approximately 15 minutes at the end of the tabletop exercise for an open discussion about the recommendations discussed in the tabletop exercise. If the attendees are tired and not contributing, the evaluator can recap some of the issues that emerged, then ask them to confirm that those issues are indeed valid. This serves as a way to check that the evaluator's initial observations are apt before they make their way into a report.

The second stage—in which the facilitator meets with the executive sponsor, high-ranking attendees, and other prominent participants—is an opportunity to gather additional feedback from a smaller and more select group of participants. This is especially important for external facilitators, as it offers a more intimate setting for feedback that may not be appropriate for all attendees.

In both stages, the facilitator has an opportunity to advocate for the interests of the participants. For example, if a discussion point revealed that the organization doesn't maintain key logs longer than 10 days and an attendee has continually advocated for funds to increase log retention, the facilitator can reinforce this recommendation in the final report. Alternatively, staff members may have repeatedly stated that they lacked training to better respond to cybersecurity events, in which case the facilitator can advocate for more training.

Sending a Survey

Within 24 hours of the tabletop exercise—when participants have had some time to reflect on the event, but it's still fresh in their minds—send them a survey via email. The purpose of this survey is partly to obtain data on the perceived efficacy of the facilitator and format, and partly to gather any thoughts participants didn't share either because there wasn't enough time or because they didn't feel comfortable. The survey should allow attendees to provide additional comments and should take no more than five minutes to complete. It can also anonymize feedback to elicit more candid comments.

The following box includes sample survey questions we've used during an exercise. For an additional sample, see the Sample Evaluation Form found in NIST SP 800-84, *Guide to Test, Training, and Exercise Programs for IT Plans and Capabilities* (*https://csrc.nist.gov/publications/detail/sp/800-84/final*).

SAMPLE SURVEY QUESTIONS

Your survey might ask participants to rate the effectiveness of the exercise and the facilitator, then rank the following statements from 1 (strongly disagree) to 5 (strongly agree):

1. The tabletop exercise was relevant to my role.
2. The tabletop exercise was relevant to my organization.
3. My participation in the exercise was warranted.
4. The facilitator kept the exercise on track.
5. The facilitator was well prepared.
6. If invited, I would participate in future tabletop exercises.
7. The tabletop exercise helped me to familiarize myself with my role during an incident.
8. The exercise helped me better understand the incident response plan.

You might also solicit short, free-form responses to questions like the following:

1. How could the organization better prepare for future tabletop exercises?
2. Are there ways the organization could improve its response to a cybersecurity incident that weren't discussed in the exercise?
3. Is there any other feedback you would like to share?

To encourage a higher response rate, the executive sponsor could be the one to send out the survey. Alternatively, you could offer the survey on paper at the conclusion of the exercise, but at that point, attendees may be fatigued and less likely to provide quality feedback. Completing a survey in person removes a degree of anonymity, which can be a negative when you're attempting to collect potentially critical feedback.

Reporting Conventions

Reporting provides proof that a tabletop exercise occurred. It may enable the organization to meet a compliance requirement or document the deficiencies or concerns identified during the exercise. This section outlines two types of reports you might create: a statement of completion and a full report.

Because these reports may be reviewed by a wide audience, ranging from an information security manager to a member of the board, they must demonstrate a high level of professionalism. To generate them, the development team should consult with the executive sponsor and legal counsel. The reports should be based entirely on facts derived from the exercise. If appropriate, they can contain direct quotes from attendees, along with recommendations grounded in best standards.

While exceptionally rare, organizations occasionally choose to forgo reporting due to budget or time restrictions or to avoid documenting tabletop exercise activities in writing. However, the benefits of reporting far outweigh the possible downsides. Even the most informal exercise will benefit from a brief statement of completion (described next), so we don't recommend forgoing this step.

Statement of Completion

Instead of a full report, an organization might create a bare-bones document memorializing a tabletop exercise, usually called a *statement of completion*. This document is nothing more than a synopsis of basic facts, including:

- Logistical information such as the date, location, and duration of the exercise
- A list of attendees and their titles
- A brief description of the scenario discussed
- A summary stating that the tabletop exercise was completed

This document, which is usually no more than two pages long, functions as proof that a tabletop exercise was performed in the event that vendors, cyber insurance underwriters, or other interested parties request such documentation.

Note that the statement of completion lacks any observations—positive or negative—drawn from the tabletop exercise. More often than not, this is by design: the organization may not want to memorialize its shortcomings for an interested external party and give them cause for concern.

Some organizations create two reports: a statement of completion and a more traditional report providing greater details that may be subject to legal and information-sharing restrictions. This allows the organization to prove to outside parties that a tabletop exercise occurred (via the statement of completion) while also providing recommendations and other opinions internally (in the detailed, protected report).

The appendix provides an example statement of completion.

Full Report

Most tabletop exercises yield a full report, which provides a full description of the exercise you conducted. In addition to the items included in the statement of completion, this comprehensive report typically contains:

- An executive summary
- A description of the scenario, including a breakdown of the scenario injects
- Specific identified deficiencies with their corresponding impacts and recommendations

If the evaluator is qualified to do so and the organization requests it, you could include the evaluator's opinion of whether the organization is prepared to address a scenario like the one explored in the exercise. However, this opinion should be built on solid ground and unquestionable to the reader.

While a tabletop exercise report length varies greatly based on the complexity of the scenario, the number of injects, and the number of recommendations, it is normally 5 to 10 pages. The reader should be able to quickly understand any identified deficiencies, so it can be helpful to break down each one into three subsections: Findings and Observations, Impact, and Recommendations.

Findings and Observations

The report should contain specific findings and observations. These could come from the evaluator in addition to the other parties who participated in the tabletop exercise, including the executive sponsor, scribe, and observers. However, the evaluator should be the ultimate arbiter of the report's contents.

Findings consist of any unexpected events that occurred during the tabletop exercise. For example, based on the organization's documentation, the development team may have expected attendees to notify the legal team when a set of facts was conveyed; however, this did not occur during the exercise. In this case, the finding would be that the attendees deviated from a documented process.

Observations are broader notes about topics that generated in-depth discussions or weren't fully explored. For example, an observation may be that attendees weren't sure if a particular vendor needed to be notified based on a set of known facts. While they ultimately chose not to notify the vendor, a decision that aligned with organizational process, the evaluator may believe the issue warrants further examination.

You should make clear how each finding and observation came to be included in the report. In other words, provide the context for how the issue emerged during the discussion. For example, if a report contained a finding stating that the organization maintained network logs for only 30 days versus the 90 days required by policy, it would be helpful to document that this issue emerged during a discussion about the organization's ability to investigate contractual requirements with a key vendor.

As an evaluator, you must also be prepared for people to dispute the facts presented in the report. To avoid this, you must ensure that all findings and observations are completely accurate and grounded in fact. You could use direct quotes from the exercise to reinforce your claim. Also, because some of the findings and observations may relate to highly technical or complicated processes, you should confer with subject matter experts to ensure that terminology, process, and jargon portray an accurate picture.

Finally, the findings and observation subsection should contain only content directly emanating from the tabletop exercise. Take care to avoid merging it with the impact or recommendations subsections.

Impact

After each finding or observation, the report should clearly articulate its impact. The impact conveys the importance of highlighting the item in the report.

Where possible, the evaluator should identify the greatest possible business impact for the organization. For example, if a network is taken offline due to a cybersecurity incident that has compromised a product-ordering system as well as automated badge-access readers for physical security, presumably the greatest business impact would be the loss of revenue resulting from the offline product-ordering system. The evaluator should avoid making fantastical claims about the impact of a particular issue, however; all statements should remain grounded in reality.

Recommendations

A recommendation is a short proposal for how to solve a particular problem. Often, recommendations will emerge during the tabletop exercise itself as the attendees brainstorm ways to alleviate a shortcoming. It most likely isn't the facilitator's role to discover a solution during the exercise, however, and the evaluator should consider whether ideas proposed by attendees appropriately address the issue.

A recommendation does not need to solve every element of an issue. For example, it doesn't need to factor in budget considerations, technical limitations, or in-depth exploration of other issues; these are for another day. It does, however, need to be realistic. Where possible, the recommendation should also be grounded in standards. Citing a standard (for example, NIST 800-61r2) adds greater weight to an argument.

EXCERPT OF A SAMPLE REPORT

These three sets of findings/observations, impacts, and recommendations were drawn from a sample report.

CLARITY SURROUNDING CONTAINMENT ACTIONS

Finding

During the tabletop exercise, the collective incident response team was unclear whether they could perform containment actions, such as severing network connectivity, on critical systems like Petroleum Pipeline 1. While the director of information security believed that he was empowered to take drastic actions and would be supported by management, this authority was not codified in any document.

Impact

During a time of crisis, all members of the incident response team should know the limits of their authority, if any. This ensures that the team doesn't take actions that may be perceived as exceeding their mandate. Furthermore, during an incident for which time is at a premium, the team should immediately understand what actions they may take to avoid wasting time during an emergency by seeking clarification from management.

Recommendation

In advance of an incident, the Cybersecurity Incident Response Plan should define the limitations of the incident response team, if any. Limitations may include not taking actions on Petroleum Pipeline 1 without the approval of the chief information officer, or other limitations set forth by the organization. This is in alignment with the guidance provided by ENISA's *Good Practice Guide for Incident Management* and NIST's *Establishing a Computer Security Incident Response Capability* (SP 800-3). Once defined, these limitations should be conveyed to members of the incident response team.

UNCERTAIN NOTIFICATION REQUIREMENTS

Finding

At Inject 2, when the incident response team determined that a cybersecurity incident had occurred, attendees were unclear who within the organization needed to be notified. Some attendees believed that they needed to immediately contact the chief executive officer, while others believed that the notification should include only the chief information officer and the legal team. After a lengthy discussion, it became clear that current processes fail to define exactly

---

who should be notified, any temporal requirements, and at what tripwires these notifications need to occur.

Impact

Involving the right people at the right time is paramount during an incident. Not doing so may impair the organization's ability to benefit from various functional skill sets, such as the legal team weighing in on the legal risks facing the organization or the communications team starting to craft internal and external statements.

Recommendation

At all times during an incident, the organization should clearly understand the severity level assigned to an incident (such as Low/Medium/High), and based on the incident categorization, notify a predefined list of contacts. This process not only saves time during an incident, as it eliminates confusion over who needs to be notified, but also ensures a consistent response. The standardization of notification processes aligns with NIST's *Computer Security Incident Handling Guide* (SP 800-61r2).

BUSINESS CONTINUITY SHORTCOMINGS

Observation

During discussions of required restoration activities stemming from a ransomware event, participants were unsure if business continuity had planned for a restoration event impacting the operational technology environment.

Impact

Because operational technology systems are a cornerstone of the business, being unable to quickly restore these systems would significantly impact the organization's customer base.

Recommendation

Confer with business continuity to determine if it has planned and tested for an event requiring the restoration of the operational technology environment.

Follow-up Activities

With the information you've learned during the exercise and the relationships built in the process, there are plenty of ways to make changes to the organization. This section focuses on some of the many follow-up activities that can occur after the exercise. Some of these are relatively quick, while others are part of a greater effort.

Assess the Incident Response Plan

A tabletop exercise focused on a cybersecurity issue is undoubtedly intertwined with the organization's incident response plan, making this a perfect time to update that plan. Using the tabletop exercise report, stakeholders should meet and discuss the plan's adequacy.

Prior to the tabletop exercise, the development team should identify the specific individual responsible for maintaining the incident response plan. While standards state that an incident response plan should have an owner, unfortunately it's not uncommon for the plan's defined owner to be "information security" or "risk management," which diffuses responsibility. The development team can work with the plan owner while developing the scenario and invite them to be a passive participant in the exercise if they already don't have a role.

Ideally, the organization's incident response plan has a predefined update interval period, such as twice a year, with out-of-cycle updates occurring as needed. The findings from the tabletop may be incorporated into the next review process; if the next update interval is several months in the future or if a critical item emerged, an ad hoc update might be appropriate.

Updates to the incident response plan aren't always arduous. Tabletop exercises might uncover several small weaknesses, such as a contact list that doesn't include phone numbers for a key vendor or a lack of clear responsibilities. Many of these are quick fixes. If a significant item emerges, however, such as uncertainty over whether the incident response team can shut down a revenue-generating application, it's possible the update will require input from several stakeholders.

Catalog and Update Other Documentation and Processes

Tabletop exercises are very likely to discuss documentation beyond the incident response plan. This might include formal policies, processes, standards, technical playbooks, and network diagrams or informal documentation such as wiki pages and intranet sites.

Following the exercise, the evaluator should catalog any documentation that may require updates, as well as gaps that require new documentation. While it isn't the evaluator's responsibility to update each document brought up during the tabletop exercise, the owners of any discussed processes should be notified of concerns so they can address them during the next update cycle.

The tabletop exercise's findings might also relate to other business processes, such as those for business continuity or risk management. For example, if a medical company determines that a security incident involving a specific system has the unexpected ability to hinder the distribution of flu vaccines (a potentially serious issue during flu season), the finding would be relevant to the organization's business impact assessment. You should weave in and communicate findings to these affected parties to increase the value of the exercise.

Conduct Follow-up Tabletop Exercises

Depending on the deficiency identified during an exercise, the remedy may involve nothing more than a few emails, or it could take months of meetings and hard work. Once the deficiencies have been addressed, it may make sense to perform a tabletop exercise focused on the remediated issues. Performing a follow-up tabletop exercise has several benefits:

- It verifies that the implemented mitigation strategies are effective.
- It triggers the creation of a new report, which can document whether the identified deficiencies were addressed.
- It demonstrates a commitment to improvement and desire to address deficiencies.

The follow-up exercise scenario doesn't need to be a complete repeat of the original scenario. It can deviate somewhat, so long as it addresses the deficiencies identified in the original exercise's report.

Implement a Formal Tabletop Exercise Program

If one doesn't already exist, the development team and executive sponsor can also develop a framework for successive events. Tabletop exercises performed quarterly or twice a year likely won't require significant planning, as each new event can be executed with a repeatable formula. You can define this tabletop exercise program in the organization's incident response plan and schedule the plan's update cycle to follow the tabletop exercises, for example.

Conducting regular tabletop exercises conveys to employees that incident response preparation is important to the organization's leadership. Tabletop exercises are an investment in one of the organization's most valuable resources: employees' time. When tabletop exercises occur on a regular basis, participating employees can observe firsthand management's commitment to reducing the risk posed by cybersecurity incidents.

If the organization has defined a formal tabletop exercise program, it should be able to perform an exercise with a few days' notice, if needed. This is extremely beneficial given that the cybersecurity threat landscape can change in a matter of hours or days due to geopolitical events, new technical exploits, or recently passed legislation. Organizations are regularly playing catch-up when responding to these landscape changes, and a tabletop exercise is one method of assessing its preparation in the face of a new threat. While details during a major event may be scarce, a snap tabletop exercise can gather key stakeholders to discuss the impact based on what is known and convey to leadership that the situation is getting due consideration.

Finally, a formalized tabletop exercise program conveys to external stakeholders that preparing for cybersecurity incidents is an important part of its information security posture. Increasingly, external stakeholders assess the cybersecurity risk of entering into a business relationship. For example, a cyber insurance underwriter will ask questions to gauge cybersecurity risk and determine the most appropriate insurance premium. By presenting a documented tabletop exercise program to interested parties, the organization proves it is taking cybersecurity seriously and making efforts to reduce risk.

Communicate High-Level Exercise Findings

Leadership is increasingly concerned about the risks caused by cybersecurity threats. After the tabletop exercise, and only with the approval of the executive sponsor, consider a process to notify leadership about the exercise and brief them on the findings. The executive sponsor can provide guidance on the appropriate forum and messaging. The executive sponsor may also be the most appropriate person to inform leadership, as they're most likely to have leadership's trust and also most aware of the nuances to convey.

The best way to inform leadership runs the gamut from a simple email to a presentation. Given that a tabletop exercise will likely reveal organizational deficiencies, filling them in during a remote or in-person meeting allows you to answer questions on the spot versus following up on long email strings. Plus, these valuable conversations could influence future tabletop exercises.

It may also be prudent to share some information about the tabletop exercise—such as the fact that it occurred, the topic, and high-level findings—with the organization's employees. Communicating this information during a regularly scheduled event, such as a quarterly all-hands call, helps reaffirm to employees that preparing for a cybersecurity incident is important to the organization. Selectively sharing a few identified shortcomings and the actions taken to remediate them will also demonstrate that the organization is making improvements as a result of the tabletop exercise. Take care to do this in conjunction with internal communications processes and in consultation with leadership and the executive sponsor. Above all, do not assign blame.

Lastly, if risk management or audit team members were unable to participate in the tabletop exercise, you may want to provide them with a copy of the report (after securing permission from the executive sponsor). Ideally, the report will demonstrate the value of the exercise and encourage these teams to participate in future events.

Identify and Analyze Trends

Once an organization has performed several tabletop exercises, it should have documentation about numerous deficiencies and recommendations, which gives it the opportunity to look for any trends across scenarios. For example, say that 7 out of 10 exercises mention that participants were confused about their responsibilities during a cybersecurity incident; this trend may point to a systemic issue that needs to be addressed. Because it's easy to focus on a singular report after a tabletop exercise, it's easy to miss the forest for the trees. Examining the reports together may reveal key information.

Summary

Some of the most valuable benefits of a tabletop exercise come after the last attendee leaves the room. By documenting the results of the exercise, an organization can prioritize action items, communicate findings with stakeholders, track improvements, and maximize the event's value.

Questions

You should understand how to evaluate the success of your tabletop exercise in advance of the event. Contemplate the following questions to decide what you'll do when the event wraps up and the organization looks to improve.

1. What are your evaluation requirements? Does a business partner, insurance provider, or other interested party expect a report?
2. Are there any reporting restrictions?
3. What type of report will you create?
4. Who will you designate as the evaluator (the person who oversees the reporting)?
5. Has anyone been tasked with addressing deficiencies, such as members of the audit or risk management teams?
6. How will participants provide feedback immediately after the tabletop exercise and in the following days?
7. How will you share the results with leadership?

PART II

EXAMPLE SCENARIOS

The next three chapters outline numerous examples of tabletop exercise scenarios that you can personalize to fit your organization. For each example, we'll provide a storyboard with injects and discussion questions. Keep in mind that these should serve only as inspiration for your tabletop exercise; you should modify these scenarios as needed to fit your environment and the goals and objectives of your exercise.

6

ENGAGING A TECHNICAL AUDIENCE

In this chapter, we focus on exercises designed to engage and challenge a technical audience, such as information technology and information security staff. Depending on the organization, participants might include team members from the security operations center and the help desk, database and network administrators, and relevant technical management, among others. Because the examples in this chapter are more technical than the example scenarios in Chapters 7 and 8, you'll need to make significant changes to address the technical nuances of your organization.

In general, the discussions that arise during a technical exercise should focus on the people, processes, and technology in place to handle the given scenario, with specific emphasis on the technological issues to address during a cybersecurity incident. However, the exercise shouldn't lose sight of the fact that technology exists to enable the business. If the developed scenario would elicit a collective "So what?" from business leaders, it's possible the exercise isn't aligned with the organization's needs.

A Widespread Phishing Campaign

Organizations frequently want to evaluate their ability to respond to large phishing campaigns, in which several users click a malicious link or engage with a suspicious email in harmful ways.

The audience for this scenario should include technical staff from the help desk, information technology, and information security teams, as well as the email administrators (if not a part of the previously listed functions). It would also be wise to involve certain members of the teams' leadership, as the scenario might require higher-level decision-making for issues impacting the business.

The Scenario

This tabletop walks through a basic phishing attack on a decentralized organization and includes an active exploitation of the environment. An *active exploitation* indicates that a threat actor is currently in the environment. Because phishing is a common threat, you could easily simplify or expand the following storyboard, adjusting it to the intended participants and their experience.

In the introduction to the scenario, the manager of the Baton Rouge location for Southwest Truck Sales, which sells large commercial vehicles, calls the help desk and says, "I think I've made a mistake. I received an email from the CEO about annual bonuses and merit increases. I downloaded the attached file, but the document is blank. I need help accessing the file."

- How will the help desk handle a call like this?
- Is the help desk trained to recognize a potential phishing attempt?
- What immediate technical steps is the help desk trained to ask the caller to perform? Are these steps adequate in this situation?
- Whom, if anyone, should this issue be escalated to, based on the single report?

Inject 1

While investigating the manager's system, the help desk receives additional calls from other Southwest Truck Sales locations reporting a suspicious email from the CEO regarding bonuses. Some users report opening a file attached to the email.

- What steps are end users trained to perform if they encounter a phishing email? In this scenario, are these steps adequate?

- Are those steps user-friendly? Are end users expected to call the help desk, or are there other ways of reporting an issue?
- Is this scenario now classified as an event or an incident?
- If it is an incident, what is its current severity level?
- Do additional parties need to be notified about the details of this issue?
- Will the help desk investigate the various tickets in concert, or will its team members operate separately?
- At this point, who oversees the investigation?
- Can the email be recovered and examined by information security personnel? Who would perform these tasks?

Inject 2

Information technology investigates the issue and finds that the email was sent to over 25 percent of the Southwest Truck Sales staff. It appears that at least 36 users from 6 locations opened the email, but whether these employees opened the attachment is unclear.

- How will the organization investigate who opened the attachment? Is the organization able to quickly make this determination?
- Can the organization query systems across the information technology infrastructure to look for evidence of the file, such as the filename or hash value?
- Is it possible to determine what, if anything, the file does upon opening, and what it contains?
- Can information technology pull the email from inboxes so that additional staff members don't open it and potentially click or download the attachment?
- Because Southwest Truck Sales has locations spread over a large geographic area, does the information technology team have the capability to examine system artifacts in real time? Can the information technology team capture data sets (such as RAM or logs) if deemed necessary?
- Does information security have the required skill sets to analyze the email and attachment? Will an outside vendor be required to provide analysis? If so, what is the process to engage them?

Inject 3

Information security investigates the attachment. After opening it, the victim is prompted to enter their domain username and password to access the sensitive contents of the malicious document. Once the credentials are entered, the document opens and appears to be blank. Information security confirms that a PowerShell script runs and downloads additional files to the system after the user enters their credentials.

During their analysis, the information security team identifies indicators of compromise (IoCs), including registry changes, MD5 hashes of specific files, and IP addresses that the compromised system attempts to contact.

- How will the compromised user credentials and the impacted systems be addressed?
- Besides the PowerShell script, are there any additional sources of information that could be used to determine if other users have been affected?
- Does the PowerShell script trigger any alerts from the organization's security tools?
- Can the remaining systems in the environment be queried to determine which ones have the malicious files? Are the registry changes, MD5 hash values, and IP addresses recorded in any system or network artifacts?

Inject 4

The investigation reveals that at least 23 systems at 5 locations have the malicious files. The systems belong to a range of users, including employees from finance, human resources, and management. Additionally, one outlier, a privileged IT administrator who has access to domain admin credentials, was compromised. Some users reported entering their credentials when prompted, but others did not remember the specific actions they took. The privileged IT administrator believed they entered their credentials but was not 100 percent sure.

- How will the organization handle the accounts of users who clicked the attachment?
- Is it possible to determine whether domain credentials have been compromised? If they are, could they be used by someone outside the corporate environment?
- Should the incident be escalated to other positions in the organization? Also, are the correct people still leading the response?
- What other evidence should be collected, and how can the response team ensure that it is properly handled?
- Is there a process to change all user account passwords across the organization, including domain admin and service account passwords, due to the potential domain admin account compromise? Can the process be executed quickly (within a few hours)? Will there be an impact on business operations?
- When was the last time a global password reset was tested or conducted?
- Do any existing network logs record activity that emanates from the systems?

Inject 5

Technical staff have reset credentials across the organization. They have reimaged impacted systems and are in the process of rebuilding them.

Based on network logs, it does not appear that further lateral movement (that is, spread throughout other parts of the network) has occurred.

- Should the organization consider implementing multifactor authentication from remote/VPN access to reduce the risk of such an attack in the future? What about for any administrative access?
- What is the process to monitor systems and the environment for reinfection post-incident?
- Are there system and network logs that can be checked for internal lateral movement or other unusual use of suspected compromised credentials?
- Who, if anyone, should be notified following the incident?
- Does this incident necessitate a formal lessons-learned process?

Possible Modifications

To adapt the scenario, consider making the following modifications:

- The email originates from a legitimate email address within the organization.
- The email originates from a legitimate partner, a vendor, or other notable external relationship.
- Lateral movement occurs, and a critical application server is accessed.
- The phishing email goes unreported.
- The email includes a link, as opposed to a file attachment. When clicked, this link may lead to a spoofed website, a file download, or another malicious site.
- The issue is widespread; for example, in a global organization, it affects three-quarters of all global sites.
- The threat actor gains access to the network and is undetected for an extended period.
- Specific logs are either available or unavailable, impacting the investigation.

Ransomware Affecting File Servers (the Technical Version)

As of this writing, ransomware continues to plague organizations globally and is the top threat for most of them. When used in a tabletop exercise, this scenario can often evolve into lengthy discussions on the best way to contain the spread, the validity of organizational backups, and whether the company has the means to restore the environment.

While a ransomware scenario can focus on both the technical and nontechnical aspects of the incident, the particular scenario we discuss here focuses on the technical ones. Other avenues of discussion, such as when to involve the cyber insurance provider and whether to pay the ransom, may emerge but shouldn't be discussed in depth in a technical exercise. Instead, save them for an executive ransomware tabletop, covered in Chapter 7.

The Scenario

In this ransomware scenario, we'll include a moderate level of exploitation of the server environment but assume that the backups and Active Directory environments remain unaffected. The threat actor will gain initial access via a phishing email and move laterally into the server farm.

The scenario begins when a staff member of Maine Pharma, a large pharmaceutical research firm, calls the help desk because they're unable to access files on their laptop. The caller has attempted to reboot, to no avail. They're frantic, as they have a big presentation later that day and can't access their slideshow.

- How will the help desk personnel handle this call? Do they remotely access the end-user system? If so, how?

- Does the help desk escalate this issue to anyone else? If so, to whom, and how?

- Given the facts known thus far, is this considered a security event or incident?

Inject 1

The help desk receives additional calls reporting similar behavior throughout Maine Pharma. Several employees report a message on their desktop demanding a ransom payment of 20 Bitcoin to a given Bitcoin wallet in exchange for access to the decryption keys and the encrypted data.

- Is the help desk trained to recognize a potential ransomware event?

- Is this now a security event or incident? What is its severity?

- Who else should be pulled into the incident at this time? How will they be notified?

- Who is leading the response?

- Is it possible to determine the extent of the spread of the ransomware?

- How can the affected endpoints be contained? Is there a tool in place that can help with the isolation process, or will it have to be done manually?

- How quickly can isolation occur? Are approvals required to isolate certain systems, and if so, how long will those approvals take?

- Should we consider isolating non-affected critical systems, such as Active Directory, backups, or other business-critical systems? (This assumes systems are not impacted yet.) If so, how will these systems be isolated?

- How will evidence found during the investigation be preserved?

Inject 2

Users are now reporting an inability to access files on numerous Maine Pharma file servers. It has been four hours since the issue was first discovered.

- Is the inability to access these systems connected to the ransomware attack?
- How can the impacted servers be checked for potential ransomware?
- How can the organization tell which systems the threat actor has gained access to?
- Has the severity of the incident increased? If so, to what level? And who else needs to be engaged?
- Can the organization get ahead of the apparent spread of activity throughout the environment?

Inject 3

Information security determines that the initial access to Maine Pharma occurred when a finance user clicked a link in a spear phishing email. This attack took advantage of an unpatched vulnerability in Microsoft Word known to be under active exploitation. Microsoft announced the vulnerability three weeks before the phishing email was sent, and a patch has been available since that announcement.

- How often are patches applied and rolled out to the organization?
- How is the organization monitoring newly announced patches, especially out-of-cycle, highly critical ones?
- Is there a process to expedite vulnerabilities under active exploitation?
- Can systems be monitored for their patch level? Is it possible to have a complete inventory of all systems that lack the relevant patches?
- What systems are in place to monitor for phishing? Is it possible to pull the phishing email from mailboxes?

Inject 4

After consultation with Maine Pharma's senior leadership, the organization determines that it will not entertain a ransom and must restore its data from available backups. Primary backups appear unaffected by the ransomware.

- How will the organization verify that the backups are safe to use?
- When was the last time backup restoration was tested?
- What needs to occur before systems can be restored and placed back into production?
- How are systems validated to ensure they are not impacted by any malware or vulnerabilities?

- How quickly can the organization restore all impacted servers to a usable state?
- Which systems will take priority in the restoration process?
- How will the restored data be reconciled?

Possible Modifications

To adapt the scenario, consider introducing the following elements:

- The organization lacks the personnel or skill sets to respond to the incident and attempt restoration.
- The ransomware has fully encrypted primary and secondary backups, rendering them unusable.
- The threat actor gains access to and encrypts the Active Directory servers or virtualization hypervisor environments.
- The threat actor has exfiltrated data and threatens to release the contents if the organization doesn't make a larger payment.
- Sensitive data, such as intellectual property or employees' health plan information, is accessed and exfiltrated.
- The organization pays the ransom and receives the encryption keys. With this modification, how long will it take for information technology to recover? How would we validate that the decryption keys or tooling function as expected?
- The ransomware has encrypted key systems, such as domain controllers, and the backups are found to be corrupted.
- The ransom payment is higher or lower than 20 Bitcoin.

A Malware Outbreak via a Zero-Day Vulnerability

In 1988, the Morris Worm spread rapidly across the internet, affecting computers across the world. As technology continues to evolve, so, too, will the attacks that organizations face. Malware outbreaks are a common occurrence in organizations, and the news is littered with examples of these widespread incidents. In this section, we cover one such event.

The malware discussed in this scenario is fictional. To make the scenario more relevant to your organization, try changing it to a variant that has recently emerged or to a fictitious version of a known piece of malware. Consider the current threat landscape as well as the business impact, and modify the scenario accordingly.

The Scenario

A new malware variant, dubbed ROBber, is spreading across organizations worldwide. The malware installs a remote access trojan and keystroke logger on infected endpoints. It then archives the logs of recorded keystrokes and sends them to a command-and-control server once a day. As the exercise begins, this information is not yet known, but it will come into play later in the exercise.

The exercise begins with Microsoft issuing an advisory regarding a zero-day vulnerability affecting systems running Internet Information Services (IIS) version 10 and below. According to the advisory, a patch is not yet available; however, Microsoft suggests immediately disabling systems running the affected versions. The advisory also included several IP addresses, which Microsoft recommends blocking. Microsoft indicates that additional details will be provided once available.

Threat groups have already started to exploit this vulnerability, and the security community has published additional advisories that involve several IoCs, including multiple IP addresses and one domain. Systems found beaconing to these addresses should be considered compromised.

Dave's Crazy Donuts, a regional breakfast chain with more than 200 stores specializing in unique donuts and coffee, runs a number of IIS systems as part of its information technology infrastructure.

- How does Dave's Crazy Donuts stay informed of security advisories and identify those that might impact its environment? Is someone on staff tasked with monitoring security advisories? Do critical advisories have a process for immediate escalation?

- How—and how quickly—would the organization respond to such an alert?

- How would the organization determine whether its systems have any IoC-related activity?

- Who is responsible for checking network traffic to the flagged IP addresses?

- How can the organization verify what, if any, systems are running IIS version 10 or earlier? How long would it take to perform this task?

Inject 1

A review of network logs within Dave's Crazy Donuts indicates irregular traffic to IP address 1.2.3.4 over SSH (TCP/22) every day at 12:22 PM. This IP address is not included in the list from Microsoft, but it is also unknown to the organization. The traffic originates from 46 different workstations and servers in the organization (representing eight restaurant locations, as well as the corporate headquarters) and is similar in nature to the traffic mentioned in the available threat posts.

- What tools are available to investigate the content of the observed TCP/22 network traffic?

- How can the company determine whether the irregular traffic stems from the vulnerability reported by Microsoft or from a separate issue?

- Is this behavior considered a cybersecurity incident? If so, what is its severity?

- Are there other parties in management or on other technical teams that must be notified about the details of this issue?

- How will the destination IP address be investigated? What about the source systems?

- What network logs are collected, and how long are they maintained? Is there a log retention policy?

- Will any containment measures be deployed? Is it typical for users to need to use SSH to access hosts on the internet, or could this service be disabled? Is there a business need to access servers and network equipment within the environment over SSH?

Inject 2

As the organization investigates the incident, it discovers 18 new systems, all containing the same 3 suspicious files, exhibiting similar behavior but beaconing to a new IP address, 1.2.3.9, also on port TCP/22. The original systems have also started sending data to this new IP address now that the previous address has been blocked.

- What actions can (and should) be taken to contain the incident now that the issue appears to be spreading rapidly?

- If information technology determines that specific containment steps are appropriate, are there limitations on shutting down certain systems that may impact restaurant operations at Dave's Crazy Donuts? Is there a documented approval process the team must undergo before taking action on those systems?

- Should the incident be escalated, either internally or externally?

- Who in the organization can investigate the suspicious files? Alternatively, should a third party come in to investigate these files? If consulting with a third party, does the organization have an incident response firm on retainer or know whom to contact?

- Are there threat intelligence sources the organization can consult to better understand the malicious files or IP addresses in use?

- Is it possible to identify the contents of the SSH connection?

Inject 3

CISA and Microsoft release a joint advisory on malware spreading at a rapid pace, dubbed ROBber. According to the report, the malware drops several files on the system, including a remote access trojan and a keystroke logger.

The hashes of the files have been included in the advisory. CISA advises that organizations block traffic to specific network blocks and disable internal versions of IIS up to and including version 10. Systems can be brought back online only after being patched or, if infected, completing specific remediation steps.

The malware also creates a logfile of the collected keystrokes in a temporary folder.

- How can the organization determine if the malware released in the advisory is the same malware affecting its systems?

- How quickly can the organization determine whether these IoCs exist on the network? How long would this process take?
- Given that the files were found at eight different restaurant locations scattered across a geographic area, is the organization able to quickly investigate the systems?
- How would the technical team understand the business implications of disabling IIS services? What alternatives could the team enact to ensure operational continuity? How long would it take to implement those contingencies?
- Legal has instructed information security to preserve the keystroke logging files in case sensitive data was captured and exfiltrated. Is this possible, and if so, what is the impact on the response efforts?
- Are there network logs that may have recorded the exfiltration of the files containing the keystrokes?

Inject 4

A quick review of the IoCs in the advisory confirms Dave's Crazy Donuts has been compromised by ROBber. Current web servers, including the main e-commerce site, are running IIS 8.5 and are all impacted by the malware. Additional systems have been infected as well.

- Given that the main e-commerce site runs many aspects of the business, including enabling customers to place orders and pick them up from their local store, would the organization disconnect the site from the internet temporarily to contain the incident? Who can authorize an action that impacts the business, and is this option technically feasible?
- If the authorized decision-maker prefers to not impact restaurant operations, how would this incident be contained?

Inject 5

It's been 24 hours since the outbreak began, and the incident appears to have been contained. No new infections have occurred, and a review of the keystroke logger's logfiles shows that it hasn't captured anything business critical or sensitive. The CEO asks for a timeline for getting all the restaurants back to full operation.

- Who certifies that the incident has been fully remediated and that restoration activities can begin?
- How will the company begin restoring systems to a known good state? In what order, and by whom?
- Does the organization have additional resources (internal or external) that can aid in the restoration process?
- How long will it realistically take to restore the systems at the various Dave's Crazy Donuts locations? Do the systems have defined recovery time objectives?

Possible Modifications

To adapt the scenario, consider making the following modifications:

- Rather than a zero-day vulnerability, the initial access vector is a phishing email, a drive-by download, an infected USB, or something else.
- The malware impacts a greater number of systems or targets other systems that may be particularly sensitive.
- The timing of the injections differs; for example, the organization first discovers anomalous traffic during routine baseline checks.
- Keystroke logfiles include sensitive information or customer data.
- The internet-bound network traffic occurs via TCP/80 or TCP/443.
- The investigation produces different IoCs than those contained in the CISA advisories, raising the question of whether the organization should share that information and, if so, how.

A Supply Chain Compromise

Compared to other cybersecurity incidents, the 2020 SolarWinds compromise was unique. SolarWinds was responsible for distributing software updates for products being used in organizations across the globe, so it had an established, trusted relationship with systems in those organizations' networks. Threat actors leveraged that trust to distribute malicious code to unsuspecting organizations, a type of attack known as a *supply chain attack.*

After the SolarWinds incident, organizations began assessing if and how they could verify the safety of software provided by third parties. The compromise also garnered considerable interest from governments due to its national security implications. One well-placed attack had impacted thousands of SolarWinds clients, including government agencies.

The following scenario imagines that a fictitious company experiences a supply chain attack via its endpoint detection and response (EDR) provider. We highly recommend modifying this scenario to involve a product currently in use in your organization's environment. As with the previous scenario, consider the current threat landscape and modify the scenario accordingly.

The Scenario

Endpoint protection company NoMoreBadStuff (NMBS) supplies EDR solutions to organizations across the globe. NMBS monitors approximately 10 percent of all the workstations in Fortune 500 companies with its NMBS EDR endpoint. A state-sponsored threat group, APT39, has gained access to NMBS's network and compromised the latest release of the EDR tool, which has been pushed to the majority of NMBS's clients.

In the introduction to the exercise, NMBS releases an advisory indicating that APT39 has compromised its build process and inserted malicious code. The compromise is limited to version 19.3 of the EDR. NMBS has since released version 19.4, which removes the malicious code, and has issued an emergency patching advisory stating that the update should be installed without delay.

Superior Automotive Parts, a large automotive parts manufacturer and distributor, is running NMBS's EDR tool on all its Windows endpoints (including servers). The company quickly becomes aware of the issue via social media.

- How often does Superior Automotive Parts review advisories? How long would it take to act upon such a notification? Are relevant staff notified of such alerts?
- How can the response team gain more insight into APT39's tactics, techniques, and procedures?
- Is it possible to inventory all systems within Superior Automotive Parts running the vulnerable version? How long would this take?
- Should the update be rolled out immediately? How can the organization determine if the new version is safe?
- Until the update is rolled out onto impacted systems, should each system be disconnected from the network? If the systems are disconnected, will this impact the update process?

Inject 1

NMBS releases additional information indicating that the malicious version created rules in the security platform to ignore APT39's toolset, enable other potentially malicious activities, and silence related alerts. Immediately following the initial installation and a time delay of 90 minutes, the compromised EDR software installs the SEAWEED backdoor on the system and connects to IP address 2.4.3.4, indicating that SEAWEED is ready for connections from threat actors.

At this time, Superior Automotive Parts is unaware of any malicious activities on its systems.

- What does the organization do with this new information from NMBS?
- Who will investigate the environment for the backdoor? What about the callback to 2.4.3.4?
- How long are network logs available for? Is there a stated policy for log retention?
- Does this new information change how the organization plans to proceed?
- Is this a cybersecurity incident, as defined by the organization's incident response plan?
- Who needs to be notified?

Inject 2

A review of network logs for the last 30 days shows that several of Superior Automotive Parts' systems have connected to the IP address 2.4.3.4. The connections occurred just two days after version 19.3 (the malicious version) was installed on all systems. Additional connections have occurred periodically since then, most recently this morning.

- Does this new revelation change the severity of the incident?
- Does this latest information change the course of action agreed upon during the scenario's introduction?
- How will the organization contain this incident?

Inject 3

Further review of network logs shows a large exfiltration of data from internal IP 192.168.4.5 over FTP. This exfiltration occurred three days ago at 5:24 AM.

- What is this system, and what data resides on it?
- How can evidence be captured on this system?
- Does the organization have the resources to collect a full disk image and memory dump from the system?
- Does the organization need to maintain a chain of custody?
- Is it possible to determine what data was exfiltrated?
- Was FTP previously blocked outbound? If so, how was this traffic allowed?

Inject 4

The CEO has requested "all hands on deck" to quickly roll out the newest version of NMBS, rebuild systems, and get the organization back online. They are requesting an ETA on this effort. In total, 43 systems have communicated with the IP address 2.4.3.4: 16 servers and 27 endpoints.

- What is the protocol for reestablishing the trust of hosts known to be compromised? Will the systems be cleaned up or restored from trusted sources?
- Based on the circumstances, what personnel does Superior Automotive Parts have to support patching the systems, removing malicious software and connections, or rebuilding systems?
- Does the organization have the personnel for around-the-clock coverage to support remediation efforts?
- Does Superior Automotive Parts work with vendors that could provide supplemental personnel on an emergency basis?
- Based on the number of impacted systems, what is the anticipated time for recovery? How are systems prioritized?
- Should passwords be reset globally? Will this include domain admins and service accounts?
- Has a global password reset ever occurred or been tested?

Possible Modifications

To adapt the scenario, consider making the following modifications:

- The threat actor is an actual adversary targeting your specific industry vertical or actively exploiting organizations at the time of the tabletop exercise.
- The organization determines that no data exfiltration occurred.
- The organization is not under active exploitation but does have the compromised software installed.
- This supply chain compromise affected a close business partner, which you could involve in the tabletop exercise.
- The IP addresses, ports, and services are specific to critical assets for your organization.
- The organization relies on a key vendor to support remediation efforts, and the vendor is unable to commit to a restoration timeline.

7

ENGAGING AN
EXECUTIVE AUDIENCE

In this chapter, we turn our attention to tabletop exercises that target an executive audience, which can include an organization's C-level employees and the leaders of various teams, such as business operations, human resources, legal, and marketing.

It isn't unusual for cybersecurity incidents, especially those that bleed into the public realm or interrupt operations, to require these cross-functional leaders to collaboratively manage the response. Unfortunately, while technical teams regularly work together, it's less common for, say, the legal and marketing teams to collaborate. For this reason, it's important to conduct regular tabletop exercises that test leadership's ability to work together in response to an incident.

Ransomware Affecting File Servers (the Senior-Level Version)

Organizations that wish to run both a technical and a senior exercise often use the same scenario, then alter the injects to fit each audience. Chapter 6 outlined a ransomware tabletop exercise meant for technical participants, and the following exercise adapts the same scenario for an executive audience. The events discussed will be similar; however, the facilitator's questions and the discussion line will focus on the business ramifications of the scenario.

The Scenario

In this ransomware scenario, the executive audience must consider strategic issues involved in the response process, such as facing business downtime, managing internal and external communications, determining whether to pay a ransom, and considering other factors. While short, the story arc contains many common strategic and high-visibility items that an executive team will be forced to contend with during a ransomware event.

Begin the scenario with users reporting that they can't access files on the Fire Lake City Schools file servers. Fire Lake City Schools is a large city school district with over 4,000 students. This issue has persisted for nearly four hours before the executive team is notified.

- How does a lack of file access impact the school district?
- What data in the file shares would pose a concern if a threat actor gained access to them?
- Given the little information available, is this a cybersecurity incident, as defined by the incident response plan?

Inject 1

Out of frustration, an employee posts several messages on social media saying that they are unable to work due to "stupid cybercriminals" who have locked them out of their computer and files. The employee has a sizable social media following, and the post immediately receives comments and shares.

- Is there a social media policy in place? Are the school district's employees aware of the policy?
- Does the post necessitate any internal or external messaging?
- How could the school district have proactively prevented the post?

Inject 2

The school district's director of information security notifies the chief information officer (CIO) of an ongoing ransomware incident in the environment. The threat actor has requested 20 Bitcoin in return for the decryption keys. The district's technical personnel are assessing whether they can use backups, but in the meantime, the information technology infrastructure remains largely inoperative.

- Does the school district have a policy on ransomware payments?
- Based on the few known details, what other information does the school district need to determine whether to even consider paying a ransom?
- Who needs to be notified and involved?
- Does the school district have the means to pay the ransom? Does it have a Bitcoin wallet, for example, or another external resource under contract that could assist with payment?
- As a public school system, is Fire Lake City Schools beholden to any laws or regulations prohibiting ransom payments? Who can help the district understand those laws or regulations?
- Should the district notify its cyber insurance provider, if there is one? Does the carrier have resources the district could bring to bear?
- Can Fire Lake's police department help? If so, how?

Inject 3

A local news outlet catches wind of the potential ransomware outbreak and calls members of Fire Lake City Schools looking for an official statement. Given that the school district is a public entity, there is considerable interest in the event. The front desk has notified the response team of these calls, as have numerous employees who have been solicited for comment.

- Who is authorized to speak to the media? Are employees aware that only approved personnel may communicate with the media?
- Is there any formal media relations training in place?
- What, if anything, will be communicated to the media outlet?
- Are there communication templates available for this and other communications, if necessary?
- Should the school district consult a media relations firm? Is a media relations firm on retainer?
- What internal communications should take place?

Inject 4

The technical teams report that they are able to restore the infected systems from clean backups. However, this entire process could take 72 to 96 hours.

- What impact does this timing have on the school district?
- Does the school district have a business continuity plan that would enable it to resume operations without its critical file shares and finance systems?

- Does this timing change any previously made decisions about the ransom?
- How will the school district decide which systems to restore first?

Possible Modifications

To adapt the scenario, consider making the following modifications:

- The amount of Bitcoin requested is significantly higher.
- The ransomware has fully encrypted primary and secondary backups, rendering them unusable.
- The threat actor contacts media outlets and informs them that the school district has been attacked.
- The threat actor has exfiltrated data and threatens to release the contents if a larger payment isn't made.
- Sensitive data, including the personally identifiable information (PII) of students and employees, is accessed and exfiltrated.
- Especially sensitive student records, such as mental health history and counseling notes, are accessed and leaked.

A Dark Web Data Discovery

Sometimes an organization doesn't realize it's been compromised until a law enforcement agency notifies it that confidential company information has been found online. On the other hand, some organizations actually employ services to monitor the dark web for their organizational secrets. In either case, if a leak occurs, the organization must determine how it lost control of the data and how to respond.

The Scenario

In this scenario, a vendor employed by the organization to perform dark web and open source intelligence monitoring discovers internal employee data for sale on the dark web. The loss of sensitive data is quickly escalated to leadership, who are forced to confront the reality that they have lost control of their data.

In the introduction, UrData, a firm specializing in sweeping various corners of the internet to look for sensitive data, spots data that appears to belong to one of their clients, Old Prairie Bank. UrData notifies Old Prairie's CIO of a dark web posting purporting to make sensitive Old Prairie data available for sale. The listing claims to include Old Prairie customer PII (names, dates of birth, addresses, account balances, and other account information). However, UrData hasn't yet obtained a sample set.

UrData informed Old Prairie's CIO that the full data set is being sold for $26,000.

- At this point, is this considered a cybersecurity incident for Old Prairie, as defined by the incident response plan?
- What actions should the CIO take upon receiving such a notification?
- Who within the organization needs to be notified?
- Does Old Prairie have an inventory of systems containing the specific customer PII? Is it possible to narrow down which systems were potentially compromised based on where PII resides?

Inject 1

UrData is able to obtain a subset of the data. The file contains the information advertised in the listing: names, dates of birth, addresses, account balances, and other basic account information.

- Do these new details change what decisions should be made?
- Who within the organization can validate that the data is indeed Old Prairie's?
- Is it possible to quickly figure out the locations where the data is stored and where the data sets originated?
- Should more people be notified and recruited to assist with the investigation, or should the response team remain small?
- Does Old Prairie have the resources to investigate such an incident? Does it need to bring in specialized vendors?
- Do any regulatory entities or other external parties need to be notified?
- Is Old Prairie required to notify its cyber insurance provider within a certain timeframe?

Inject 2

UrData has negotiated the price of the data set down to $11,200 in Bitcoin, but the parties selling the data will honor this price only for the next eight hours.

In researching the sellers, UrData has determined there is a small chance that the group is associated with North Korea.

- Will Old Prairie entertain purchasing the data set at the reduced price?
- Does the fact that the group is possibly associated with North Korea, a country that may be under regulatory scrutiny, impact the bank's decision of whether to purchase the data set?
- What value would purchasing the data set provide?
- Who makes the decision to pay, and how would the transaction be performed? How quickly could Old Prairie attain Bitcoin?

Inject 3

Old Prairie decides to pay, and UrData obtains the full data set. A review of the data and its format confirms the data is a direct export from Old Prairie's MyOP customer database. It appears to be roughly one month old.

- Who has direct access to the MyOP database and could have exfiltrated this data? Do any external parties have access to the MyOP data?
- Is there a chance that an external threat actor has access to the network?
- Has Old Prairie engaged its legal counsel?
- Based on the type and amount of data exfiltrated, what regulatory agencies or external parties (such as customers) must be notified? Does Old Prairie have a vendor that can assist with these notifications?
- Assuming that Old Prairie will need to publicly disclose the loss of customer data, what additional vendors or personnel (for example, a crisis management team) should it involve?
- Are the company employees aware of the leak? If so, how does this impact the response process?

Inject 4

The organization suspects Jan, a database administrator recently passed over for a promotion, of being involved in the data exfiltration. Investigation of the system logs at the time in question shows that Jan's account accessed and downloaded large amounts of data from multiple databases.

- What is the process for handling the evidence found during the investigation?
- Is it possible to quickly terminate Jan's access? If so, who makes this decision?
- Who on the team is responsible for discussing this evidence with Jan? How will that process be handled?
- What is the role of the human resources team in the response?
- Should law enforcement be contacted? Who determines this, and who performs the contact if applicable? What agency should be contacted?
- Is there an existing process for handling insider threat situations like the one in this scenario?

Possible Modifications

To adapt the scenario, consider making the following modifications:

- The amount requested for the data set is significantly higher.
- There is a high, not low, likelihood that North Korea is involved, whose government is sanctioned by the United States, and Old Prairie may need to seek additional guidance.
- The compromised information is partner data, unreleased earnings, or any other sensitive data the organization maintains.

- The scenario proceeds with Jan either denying the allegations or confirming them.
- An external threat actor had access to the environment or perhaps still does and is actively exfiltrating data.
- The data set is posted to a publicly available source, such as Pastebin.
- The threat actors sold fictitious data that isn't connected to Old Prairie. This requires Old Prairie to conduct further investigations to prove that a data loss *didn't* occur.
- The data set provided by the attackers is older than six months, causing Old Prairie to consider what investigatory artifacts are available.

A Distributed Denial-of-Service Attack

As the threat landscape continues to evolve, so do the types of attacks we see happening. Distributed denial-of-service (DDoS) attacks have been around for some time, but ransom-based DDoS attacks, like the one we explore here, are increasing in popularity. It's important to understand how to respond to this unique attack type, as well as how your organization can continue to operate in the event of a prolonged attack. Executing a tabletop exercise to discuss a DDoS attack is one way to test organizational capabilities.

The Scenario

In this scenario, a DDoS attack affects an online lender's website functionality. Any organization with a web presence could adapt this scenario to fit its use case, though it would be particularly impactful for organizations whose business is conducted through their website (compared to those that merely use their website to provide public information).

Begin with the web team for QuickPaydayLoans.net discovering an outage of its external website that affects all functionality, including loan applications, bill pay, transfers, and account access. The lender's public-facing informational website is also impacted.

- Will the web team be notified of an accessibility issue impacting the website or learn about it by other means? How long will this take? Who will likely be the first party to recognize there was a DDoS attack?
- Who should investigate these issues?
- What is the escalation and notification process, internally and externally?
- How long can an outage last before the public should be notified?

Inject 1

An investigation by the web team finds that a DDoS attack caused the outage. According to the CIO, the team is working with the lender's internet service provider but doesn't know how long the issue will take to resolve. It's been 90 minutes since the outage started.

- Does this new information change the severity of the incident?
- Who should be engaged and notified now, both internally and externally?
- Are there other issues to worry about?
- How long can the lender operate without these services available? Does it need to worry about customer fallout?
- When was the last time the lender conducted a business continuity or disaster recovery review? Has the business continuity plan been tested?
- Does the lender have a relationship with a DDoS mitigation provider? If not, how quickly can the lender establish one?

Inject 2

The outage is ongoing, and the web team and internet service provider have been unable to mitigate the attack as the threat actor continues to employ new IP addresses. It's now been six hours, and local news outlets have caught wind of the issue. One outlet suggests that the lender is the latest in a string of organizations affected by the threat actor APT38.

- Who is authorized to speak to the media?
- Is the lender aware of what and what not to say to the media?
- Have employees received any formal media relations training?
- What, if anything, will the lender communicate to media outlets?
- Are there communication templates available for this and other communications, if necessary?
- Should the lender consult with a media relations firm?

Inject 3

Customers have grown frustrated and concerned over the safety of their information and finances. The lender has had several customer inquiries, and it's clear that customer confidence is shaken.

- How can the lender communicate the cause of the outage to customers, and how does it maintain its reputation?
- What channels can it use to communicate externally?
- Who internally is responsible for crafting these communications?
- If customers are unable to make loan payments, potentially for several days, what is the financial impact on the company?
- If a customer can't make payments by a deadline due to the incident, will the organization be unable to charge late fees?

Inject 4

The threat actor contacts the lender and says that it will halt the attack if paid 46 Bitcoin; otherwise, the attack will continue.

- Should the lender consider paying the ransom?
- How does the lender know that the attack will stop if it pays?
- Can the lender mitigate the attack so it doesn't need to pay? What will this take, and how much will it cost?

Inject 5

The attack has ceased; however, the board of directors would like an immediate update about why this attack happened and what can be done to protect the lender from future attacks.

- What technologies or resources are available to mitigate such an attack?
- What research does the incident response team need to conduct before reporting to the board?

Possible Modifications

To adapt the scenario, consider making the following modifications:

- The ransom payment is significantly higher or lower.
- The threat actor doesn't make a ransom request.
- The attack is sporadic rather than constant.
- The attack goes on for days and impacts the ability to process financial transactions.
- The attack takes down multiple internal and external services, completely incapacitating the lender.
- The threat group is an established adversary specifically targeting the payday loan industry.

8

ENGAGING THE BUSINESS

Sometimes it can be hard to explain to nontechnical staff that they, too, have a role to play in a cybersecurity incident. In this final chapter, we focus on exercises designed to engage specific groups within the business— namely, physical security, communications, and human resources.

While these scenarios might also involve information technology and information security staff, we've designed them to show an organization that incident response involves more than just technical responders. An organization feels the real impact of a cybersecurity incident when it affects the business.

A Physical Security Breach

It's easy to forget that information security incidents can stem from security failings in the physical world. In fact, a threat actor who breaches the physical security of a building can cause just as much damage, if not more, as an attacker compromising the information technology network from abroad.

One of the benefits of exploring such a scenario is that it involves a team not typically included in an information security tabletop: physical security. Some organizations might not even have such a role, instead placing the responsibility of securing the property to risk management or another unrelated function.

A physical security breach can certainly be far-fetched and resemble scenes from a *Mission: Impossible* movie (picture a threat actor crawling through heating and cooling air ducts). But even a simple attack can cause headaches, as in the example we outline here.

The Scenario

A threat actor gains access to a physical building by circumventing security controls. While in the building, they're relatively unimpeded and have free rein to explore the facility. After some time, they leave with several items of value, including laptops, external storage devices (such as hard drives), and documents.

In the exercise introduction, the threat actor is dressed in business casual clothing and enters the lobby of the corporate headquarters for MedCo, a medical insurance company. In order to proceed, the threat actor must present an access card to a radio-frequency identification (RFID) reader, which grants access and unlocks the door.

At 8:30 AM, when foot traffic is greatest for employees arriving at MedCo to start their workday, the threat actor fumbles around in their backpack until a MedCo employee uses their card to enter, causing the RFID reader to beep and unlock the door. The threat actor smiles and gestures to indicate that they found their card, pulling a similarly colored access card out of their backpack. They pass it over the RFID reader (which does not beep) and grab the door as it is closing.

The threat actor now has access to MedCo's secure facility.

- Do MedCo employees undergo training on physical security access threats (such as tailgating, which occurred here)? If so, what are employees trained to do?

- Would a security guard, camera, or other monitor have observed this inappropriate access?

- Who is responsible for the physical security of the facility?

Inject 1

Posing as an employee of MedCo, the threat actor sits at a desk meant for visiting remote employees. They pull out a laptop and plug the available network cable into their laptop, then attempt to connect to the network.

- Is there an authentication process that the laptop must undergo to connect to the organization's network? What MedCo resources could the threat actor have reasonably accessed?

- Would the information security team be alerted to the presence of an unknown information system connecting to the network? Would any other alerts be tripped?

Inject 2

The threat actor walks up to an administrative assistant's desk and states, "I'm with Phil & Son's HVAC Systems. We had an appointment to perform a maintenance check on the server room's HVAC system. Can you let me in? Dave should know I'm coming." The threat actor has a small bag of tools and appears, at first glance, to be an HVAC technician. Dave is MedCo's IT manager, and his information is easy to find on LinkedIn.

- What process does a contractor need to follow to request access to a system or room?
- Is there a unique process for requesting access to sensitive rooms, such as the one containing servers?
- Are MedCo employees encouraged or discouraged to share their employment information on social media?

Inject 3

The administrative assistant asks the threat actor to take a seat while she wisely checks with information technology. The threat actor excuses themselves to use the restroom. Concerned that they may be discovered, they make their way to the exit.

Before leaving, the threat actor collects three laptops from unattended cubicles, places them in a backpack, and walks out the door.

- Assuming the employees discover that their laptops are missing when they return to their cubicles, is there a designated process in place for them to report the theft?
- In the past, have employees used this designated process?
- Are there security cameras in the lobby, parking lot, working areas, or other locations? If so, how long is their footage retained?
- What methods are in place to track stolen or lost MedCo assets?

Inject 4

The threat actor leaves the facility and drives away. The employees who are missing their laptops alert information security, which quickly notifies physical security.

- If the threat actor closes the laptop before leaving or powers it down, is it possible for them to later access its contents? If so, how?
- How long would it take to determine the identifying information (such as serial numbers) of the stolen laptops? Would the organization be able to determine (a) if the device was encrypted and (b) what sensitive information was on the device?

- Is it possible to remotely disable or wipe the devices?
- Is there a process in place for notifying law enforcement?
- If the laptops contain sensitive data, should other MedCo parties, such as the legal team, be notified of the loss?
- If cameras are in place, how long are the recordings maintained? Would security cameras be able to reconstruct the threat actor's movements in the facility?

Possible Modifications

To adapt the scenario, consider making the following modifications:

- The threat actor is an ex-employee with intimate knowledge of how to navigate the facility.
- The threat actor steals data (contained on laptops or external hard drives) that is extremely sensitive and necessitates a significant response.
- The threat actor attains a more significant beachhead into the organization's network.
- The threat actor poses as a member of the help desk team, pretends that there's an issue at a workstation, and requests access to the employee's system.
- The threat actor enters the facility after hours, pretending to be a member of the cleaning crew.
- The threat actor causes a disruption to the environment, either virtually or by physically tampering with network equipment.
- The threat actor installs a physical device in the environment, such as a rogue Wi-Fi access point mimicking a legitimate signal.

A Social Media Compromise

Organizations use social media accounts to varying degrees. For some, these accounts are their primary mechanism for communicating with customers (and potentially employees). Social media also enables organizations to curate their brand image, which could take years to develop. The following scenario is most appropriate for these social media–forward companies.

Because a social media compromise is public facing from its initial moments, responding to it requires increased urgency. More importantly, it requires collaboration between teams that don't typically work closely together, such as information security and the team that is responsible for social media (usually marketing). And, as you might discover, it isn't uncommon for the marketing team to run its social media accounts without information security controls like multifactor authentication and password hygiene requirements.

The Scenario

In this scenario, a threat actor posts to the organization's social media accounts. Though simple, this exercise can quickly generate discussion about a myriad of pressing concerns and an incident bubbling into the public domain. Because the organization has lost control of the account and can't log in, staff must quickly determine how to (a) regain control of the accounts and (b) communicate with a public concerned about the content of the posts.

Begin at 3 AM on Saturday morning, when Happy Bear Childcare Centers, a regional childcare facility with over 150 locations in Canada and almost 4,000 full- and part-time employees, finds that its social media feeds have been populated with propaganda from the Levant Liberation Army.

The propaganda includes derogatory messages about various parties, along with several other offensive statements. The messages contrast starkly with Happy Bear Childcare Centers' previous social media messages promoting their business.

- At 3 AM on the weekend, is any member of Happy Bear's staff monitoring the social media platforms?
- Has Happy Bear hired a social media brand reputation company, which may have seen the messages from the Levant Liberation Army? If so, what is the process for alerting staff?
- How long will it likely be until staff discovers the messages?

Inject 1

Alerted to the posts by observant employees, Happy Bear's marketing staff attempts to log in to the accounts, remove the content, and change the password. In doing so, the staff realizes that the password has been changed and they're unable to log in.

- Is this event a cybersecurity incident, as defined by Happy Bear's incident response plan (if there is one)?
- Who within the organization should be contacted for assistance? Who else must be informed?
- Is there a process for recovering passwords from social media accounts?

Inject 2

The Happy Bear marketing staff attempts to regain control of the social media accounts via the provider's Recover Account option. The social media provider tells the staff it will take 24 to 48 hours before the accounts are restored.

NOTE *In a real-world situation, it's unlikely to take this long to recover accounts. However, introducing the time delay adds further stress to the scenario.*

- Knowing that the derogatory messages will remain broadly visible for another day or two, how should Happy Bear respond?
- What is the process for getting support from social media outlets for issues like this, where login credentials are not working, as well as for other support-related questions? Is this process documented?
- Are there alternative channels, whether social media based or otherwise, that enable Happy Bear staff to communicate to parents and other concerned parties?
- Is there a process, documented or otherwise, to create and approve communications to clients, staff, and the public?
- Does Happy Bear have a crisis management firm on retainer that can expeditiously assist with the communications?

Inject 3

The threat actors proceed to post more derogatory messages. Additionally, they publish a post demanding $50,000 in Bitcoin from the organization in exchange for releasing the accounts; otherwise, they threaten, they will distribute student information they have allegedly stolen. Some of the information contains sensitive medical information for students with special needs.

- Would Happy Bear entertain paying the ransom?
- Does Happy Bear have cyber insurance that could cover the costs of any reputational damage, as well as the ransom payment?
- How should Happy Bear staff interact with the attackers?
- How should Happy Bear staff interact with concerned parents?
- If the student information was indeed stolen, what regulatory authorities should be notified, and by when?
- Should law enforcement be contacted? If so, what assistance would they likely be able to provide?

Inject 4

Happy Bear's CEO, increasingly concerned about the public fallout and release of sensitive data, has requested that an incident response team investigate whether a compromise has occurred.

- Does Happy Bear have an existing relationship with an incident response firm?
- Who will lead and direct the investigation? What are its goals?

Inject 5

The posts have gained notoriety on the internet, and the media has contacted Happy Bear for comment. A national news channel plans to run a segment about cybersecurity and will highlight the impact of the incident on innocent children and concerned parents.

- Has anyone been assigned ahead of time to speak to the media? What is the process for selecting such a representative?
- Is there a cyber insurance policy in place that can aid Happy Bear in restoring its brand?
- Is there a media relations firm on retainer that could assist Happy Bear with external media communications?

Inject 6

Happy Bear regains access to the social media accounts and promptly deletes the material. The unwanted posts remained up for a total of 36 hours.

- How will Happy Bear respond now that the accounts are under its control?
- What immediate steps will it take to secure the social media accounts before it can establish a long-term solution?
- How will Happy Bear address the threat actors' statement that sensitive information was compromised?

Inject 7

The incident response team provides the preliminary results of its investigation, which includes an examination of the process breakdowns that led to the compromise. The team determines that the social media accounts weren't secured with multifactor authentication and that multiple employees shared a simple password. These practices do not align with Happy Bear's information security policy.

Furthermore, the attacker captured the credentials after a marketing employee clicked a phishing email. The marketing employee had failed numerous phishing tests and consistently neglected to follow safe computing practices. The incident response team also determined that there was no evidence of data exfiltration.

- What is the human resource team's role in the investigation?
- Even if the incident response team found no evidence of data exfiltration, do regulatory authorities need to be notified?
- How will Happy Bear notify parents to reassure them that no information was lost? What can the company do to reestablish trust?
- Assuming the company issues a final report, who is responsible for implementing corrective actions?

Possible Modifications

To adapt the scenario, consider making the following modifications:

- The allegedly exfiltrated data set belongs to the organization conducting the exercise, and if lost, it would cause significant concern in the public.

- The threat actor presents a sample of stolen information, leading the organization to believe the data was indeed stolen.

- The incident response team finds evidence that sensitive data really was stolen, necessitating a greater response.

- Parents or other affected individuals threaten litigation, causing the organization to take protective legal actions.

- The stolen sensitive data belongs to a multinational client base, complicating regulatory notification issues.

- The organization is publicly traded, and the loss of data has a material impact on its finances, requiring the company to notify additional parties.

An Insider Threat

Most organizations make security investments focused on keeping themselves safe from external threat actors, but insider threats are an equally consequential possibility that tabletop exercises should explore.

Insider threats take many forms: lackadaisical employees failing to take security seriously, employees determined to cause harm to their employer, or staff who want to profit from the sale of intellectual property, to name a few.

If you've engaged an outside consultant for an insider threat scenario, it's especially important to leverage a trusted agent from the organization to help you craft a realistic scenario. Most insider threats occur when employees abuse their previously granted privileges, and a trusted agent is more likely than the facilitator to understand these potential control breakdowns.

During the scenario, be sure to contemplate both technical and non-technical threats. The internet is filled with stories about sensitive data being lost simply because someone stole printouts or took pictures of data with a cell phone camera.

Finally, while the scenario will likely involve technical controls, various policies and procedures might also come into play, requiring legal or other teams to get involved.

The Scenario

Mica's Fleet Repair, which repairs large commercial automotive fleets, provides a highly customized service. One of its most valuable assets is its extensive list of customer contacts, which includes the individualized pricing offered to each customer. Many businesses face the following scenario:

an insider steals key intellectual property with the intention of opening a competing business.

Begin the scenario when David, a longtime account manager at Mica's Fleet Repair, finishes a meeting with one of Mica's original clients, Central Delivery Services. Central had recently decided to end its relationship with Mica's. When asked why, Central responded that it was happy with Mica's services, but it had received a quote that was 10 percent cheaper from NYFleet, a new upstart formed by a former Mica employee, Ajay.

Much to David's frustration, this was the fifth client Mica's had recently lost due to a bid that was almost exactly 10 percent cheaper. David suspects that Ajay may have taken information with him when he left.

- Is there a process for reporting the suspected theft of intellectual property? To whom should it be reported?
- Is this a cybersecurity incident, as defined by Mica's incident response plan?
- Who must be informed?

Inject 1

The loss of accounts is troubling enough that it gains the attention of Mica's executive management, which suspects that Ajay may have left with Mica's intellectual property, such as pricing lists and contracts. Mica's legal counsel starts to examine the facts around Ajay's departure, as well as Mica's separation process.

- Is there a separation process through which Mica's debriefs employees prior to their last day?
- At their hiring and at regular intervals afterward, are employees informed of policies regarding sensitive information?
- Is sensitive information labeled as such, and have additional security controls been implemented to protect it?
- Is there a unique departure process for employees who had access to sensitive information?

Inject 2

Mica's legal counsel requests information about the location of all sensitive account information, including contracts, key contacts, and other data.

- Does the organization define a data classification schema that clearly delineates sensitive business information and information that doesn't need protection?
- Is there an inventory of all sensitive account information and its locations?
- Are access controls in place to limit access to that data and record which users have accessed it?

Inject 3

Mica's information technology staff reports that much of the sensitive account information is stored in one system and that Ajay, along with 30 other account managers, had access to it.

- Do logs record each account manager's logins, along with the activities they performed? How long are the logs maintained?
- Do existing controls prevent users from downloading sensitive business information or transferring it outside the network (via email, for example)?

Inject 4

Mica's legal counsel asks that the information technology team provide an inventory of the information systems that Ajay used during his employment. They would like to preserve any of Ajay's information in case it becomes relevant for investigatory purposes and potential litigation.

- What is the process for receiving a terminated employee's computer, phone, or other devices?
- How long are devices stored before being reissued or destroyed?
- Before being reissued to a new employee, are the devices wiped?

Inject 5

A former colleague of Ajay's, Martin, approaches his manager after hearing rumors that Ajay is being investigated. Martin tells his manager that Ajay once bragged about how easy it would be to email client information to himself and start his own competing business. It has been four months since Ajay's departure.

- How long does Mica's maintain email accounts following an employee's departure? Is there a retention or destruction policy?
- After four months, what remaining investigatory artifacts could help verify whether Ajay emailed himself the documents?

Inject 6

As the investigation unfolds, it becomes clear that a number of policy and technology breakdowns would have enabled Ajay to steal intellectual property. Executive management wants to make changes so this does not happen again.

- Given that the breakdown occurred across teams, should a certain role take the lead in addressing it? If so, who? Perhaps audit or risk management?
- How will Mica's validate that the identified gaps have been corrected? Who, specifically, can determine that the implemented solutions are adequate?

Possible Modifications

To adapt the scenario, consider making the following modifications:

- The vector used to steal sensitive information includes printing documents, using a cell phone camera, or downloading files to a USB drive.
- The sensitive information is relevant to the organization conducting the exercise. For example, it may include chemical formulas, prototype drawings, or research data.
- Instead of losing client information, the insider stole regulated data (such as health information) or information that necessitates notifying other businesses.
- The insider is a current employee, and their role makes them highly knowledgeable about information technology processes. This means they are capable of covering their tracks by deleting logs. (Also, if the departure of such an employee would cause significant hardships, discuss during the exercise the possibility of making some employee tasks redundant to ensure that power and knowledge don't reside solely with one person.)

APPENDIX

REPORTING TEMPLATES

This appendix provides examples of a statement of completion and a full report for a tabletop exercise performed at a bank. We encourage you to adapt the format of these reports to fit your organization's style and needs. Throughout this appendix, the text in italics is for guidance and should not be included in the report. For more information about the tabletop exercise reporting process, see Chapter 5.

Statement of Completion Template

Describe the purpose of the exercise, including any compliance obligations.
Old Prairie Bank performed a tabletop exercise to explore incident response issues related to a cybersecurity incident. The tabletop exercise

satisfied the requirement, defined in the incident response plan, to test the plan's processes annually.

Describe the time and location of the exercise and the duration of its planning.

Planning commenced in June of 2024 and culminated with the performance of the tabletop exercise on September 23, 2024, at Old Prairie's headquarters, located at 22 Jefferson Street, St. Joseph, Missouri.

List all members of the development team.

The development team, which created and facilitated the tabletop exercise, included:

- Ruth Miller, Vice President of Information Technology
- Michelle Kane, Vice President of Communications

List all attendees.

The attendees of the tabletop exercise included:

- Megan Tibbs, Vice President of Digital Banking
- Joanne Svenningsen, Director of Finance
- Janice Marquardt, Director of Risk Management
- Sheryl Shectman, Director of Information Technology
- Corina Milea, Director of Human Resources

List the exercise's objectives. In this report example, the goal is the completion of the exercise itself, which contains several objectives.

The objectives of the exercise were to:

- Gain an understanding of employees' roles and responsibilities during a cybersecurity incident.
- Improve communication and collaboration across the cybersecurity incident response team.
- Practice the organization's response to a realistic cybersecurity incident by following the cybersecurity incident response plan.

Scenario Description

Provide a short description of the scenario and each inject. For the statement of completion, you may choose to include a brief paragraph summarizing the scenario instead of the individual injects.

The scenario presented during the tabletop exercise involved a social media compromise and extortion. It contained the following injects:

1. An external threat actor compromises Old Prairie's Facebook and X accounts. The accounts now display propaganda from a well-known terrorist group.
2. When attempting to change the content on their social media pages, employees learn that they're locked out of the accounts and unable to make changes.

3. Local media groups and concerned customers contact Old Prairie about the posted content.

4. The threat actor posts several messages claiming they have stolen personal information, including bank account records, from Old Prairie. The messages demand payment in Bitcoin to avoid the release of data.

5. Old Prairie regains control of the social media accounts.

6. Old Prairie's information security staff finds no evidence that the attack went beyond the social media accounts and believes it's unlikely that personal data was compromised.

7. The investigation determines that a member of Old Prairie's marketing team clicked a phishing email, which compromised usernames and passwords. This employee has a history of clicking phishing links.

Summary

Describe the participants' attendance, engagement, and debrief activities.
All attendees were present for the duration of the exercise (which lasted more than two hours) and actively participated. At the conclusion, the facilitator held a short debrief session to gather feedback and identify additional process improvements, which we'll evaluate for inclusion during the next incident response plan update cycle.

Full Report Template

In addition to the elements contained in the statement of completion, a full report contains an executive summary, which leadership can use to quickly understand why a tabletop exercise occurred and what deficiencies it uncovered. This executive summary should make sense to the reader without any additional information. The full report should also list the specific findings and observations, with their corresponding impacts and recommendations. Finally, it should include a short section itemizing any areas of success.

Executive Summary

Describe the purpose of the exercise, including any compliance obligations.
Old Prairie Bank performed a tabletop exercise to explore incident response issues related to a cybersecurity incident. The tabletop exercise satisfied the requirement, defined in the incident response plan, to test the plan's processes annually.

Describe the time and location of the exercise and the duration of its planning.
Planning commenced in June of 2024 and culminated with the performance of the tabletop exercise on September 23, 2024, at Old Prairie's headquarters, located at 22 Jefferson Street, St. Joseph, Missouri.

List the exercise's objectives. In this report example, the goal is the completion of the exercise itself, which contains several objectives.
The objectives of the exercise were to:

- Gain an understanding of employees' roles and responsibilities during a cybersecurity incident.
- Improve communication and collaboration across the cybersecurity incident response team.
- Practice the organization's response to a realistic cybersecurity incident by following the cybersecurity incident response plan.

Provide a short description of the scenario.
The exercise's scenario involves a threat actor gaining control of Old Prairie's Facebook and X accounts, posting disparaging and unwanted content, and threatening to release stolen data unless a ransom is paid.

List process deficiencies.
The tabletop exercise uncovered several deficiencies in Old Prairie's processes. These included:

- Poor password hygiene for Old Prairie's social media accounts that conflicts with the organization's password policies
- A lack of awareness of defined roles and responsibilities for Old Prairie staff during a cybersecurity incident
- A lack of legal counsel (whether on staff or retained) able to determine whether Old Prairie needs to perform notifications, and to what jurisdiction, when sensitive data is lost

Evaluate the severity of identified process deficiencies.
While none of the identified deficiencies is particularly severe, they present opportunities to reduce the risk of the organization's social media accounts being compromised and to improve the efficiency of the incident response process.

Describe the plan to address the identified deficiencies.
Relevant stakeholders will examine the identified deficiencies and test any fixes during a follow-up tabletop exercise to ensure the issues were remediated.

Overview

List all members of the development team.
The development team, which created and facilitated the tabletop exercise, included:

- Ruth Miller, Vice President of Information Technology
- Michelle Kane, Vice President of Communications

List all attendees.

The attendees of the tabletop exercise included:

- Megan Tibbs, Vice President of Digital Banking
- Joanne Svenningsen, Director of Finance
- Janice Marquardt, Director of Risk Management
- Sheryl Shectman, Director of Information Technology
- Corina Milea, Director of Human Resources

List the exercise's objectives.

The objectives of the exercise were to:

- Gain an understanding of employees' roles and responsibilities during a cybersecurity incident.
- Improve communication and collaboration across the cybersecurity incident response team.
- Practice the organization's response to a realistic cybersecurity incident by following the cybersecurity incident response plan.

Scenario Description

Provide a short description of the scenario and each inject.

The scenario presented during the tabletop exercise involved a social media compromise and extortion. It contained the following injects:

1. An external threat actor compromises Old Prairie's Facebook and X accounts. The accounts now display propaganda from a well-known terrorist group.
2. When attempting to change the content on their social media pages, employees learn that they're locked out of the accounts and unable to make changes.
3. Local media groups and concerned customers contact Old Prairie about the posted content.
4. The threat actor posts several messages claiming they have stolen personal information, including bank account records, from Old Prairie. The messages demand payment in Bitcoin to avoid the release of data.
5. Old Prairie regains control of the social media accounts.
6. Old Prairie's information security staff finds no evidence that the attack went beyond the social media accounts and believes it's unlikely that personal data was compromised.
7. The investigation determines that a member of Old Prairie's marketing team clicked a phishing email, which compromised usernames and passwords. This employee has a history of clicking phishing links.

Findings and Observations

Describe the process of soliciting feedback.

The tabletop exercise concluded with a debrief that included all attendees. Later, a smaller group of key stakeholders performed a second debrief. The development team solicited feedback from both groups about potential improvements and other concerns. In addition, participants completed a post-exercise survey. The following sections summarize the resulting feedback, as well as observations made during the tabletop exercise itself.

Describe any strengths identified during the tabletop exercise.

The exercise revealed the following areas of success:

Collaboration

This tabletop exercise highlighted the tremendous teamwork at Old Prairie. All attendees actively engaged with the exercise, expressed their opinions, and worked toward a successful end to the incident, even when they lacked knowledge of incident response.

External partnerships

The technical team's partnership with several external firms, including an external incident response team and a cyber insurance partner, will help any major incident response effort.

Commitment of senior management

Old Prairie's senior management devoted over two hours to participating in the tabletop exercise and post-exercise debrief, proving their commitment to the process.

Describe any identified issues in detail, including findings and observations, their impacts, and any recommendations for improvement.

We also identified several weaknesses, listed here, along with recommendations for their improvement.

Improperly Managed Social Media Passwords

Old Prairie's password management policy (Policy #201b) defines authentication requirements for all accounts in the Old Prairie environment and any external account that contains Old Prairie data. Of particular interest, Policy #201b states:

- All passwords will contain at least 15 characters, numbers, or symbols.
- All passwords will be changed at a frequency of once every six months.
- Passwords will not be shared between employees of Old Prairie.
- Multifactor authentication, if available, must be enabled.
- All deviations from Policy #201b require the written approval of Old Prairie's Chief Information Security Officer.

During the exercise, it was determined that:

- At least three employees shared a single password to Old Prairie's social media accounts.
- Employees used the same password for two social media accounts.
- It was possible for a single employee to lock out the other employees by changing the passwords of the social media accounts.
- The password was an easy-to-guess dictionary word without unique symbols, numbers, or capitalization.
- Multifactor authentication, while available, wasn't enabled.

While the participants were aware of Policy #201b, they didn't understand its applicability to Old Prairie's social media accounts.

Impact

The identified poor password practices make it easier for threat actors to harm the organization. A compromise of Old Prairie's Facebook and X (formerly Twitter) accounts could significantly impact Old Prairie's reputation and concern its customer base.

Recommendations

Old Prairie should reexamine Policy #201b and confirm its applicability to social media and other accounts. After performing any necessary updates, Old Prairie should educate all employees about the policy's scope. Finally, Old Prairie should update all social media accounts to conform to Policy #201b. Old Prairie should periodically audit both internal and external accounts to ensure policy compliance.

Insufficient Knowledge of Data Loss Notification Requirements

According to Old Prairie's cybersecurity incident response plan, the organization's general counsel is responsible for spearheading data loss notifications to the impacted party and regulatory authorities. During the scenario, the general counsel expressed some familiarity with Missouri's data breach notification laws but was unfamiliar with those of neighboring states, where some of Old Prairie's customer base resides. Comments from Old Prairie staff suggested that the organization doesn't currently possess the expertise needed to determine the steps to take during a data loss incident.

Impact

A cybersecurity incident may require the swift notification of key regulatory authorities within a defined time period. Without knowledge of data breach laws for relevant jurisdictions, Old Prairie might not be able to perform these notifications in a timely manner. During a cybersecurity incident, when time is valuable, the organization may be forced to waste precious time seeking and procuring appropriate legal resources.

Recommendations

Old Prairie's general counsel should seek out, evaluate, and retain a law firm with expertise in data breach notification for the entire United States.

Lack of Understanding of Roles During an Incident

The cybersecurity incident response plan describes the roles and responsibilities of staff members during an incident. However, few employees were aware of their specific obligations. During the tabletop exercise, the facilitator asked participants about the actions they would take while responding to a cybersecurity incident. It was rare for these actions to align with those defined in the cybersecurity incident response plan, and in several instances, staff members recommended actions that directly contradicted the plan. When prodded, the majority of attendees admitted that they weren't aware of the plan's contents.

Impact

All organizations seeking to respond comprehensively to an incident must perform incident response planning. While Old Prairie has a cybersecurity incident response plan, employees lack knowledge of it, which might unnecessarily prolong a response. If stakeholders ignore the plan, they might improperly perform important steps.

Recommendations

Old Prairie staff with roles in the incident response plan should be familiar with their responsibilities during a cybersecurity incident. Old Prairie should educate its entire staff on the existence of the plan and dedicate smaller training sessions for employees with roles.

Conclusion

Describe opportunities for improvement and next steps.

Old Prairie's tabletop exercise revealed several opportunities for improvement. Some security shortcomings provide fertile ground for an incident (such as poor social media password practices and policy awareness), while others could hinder the organization's ability to respond to an incident promptly (such as a lack of awareness of roles and responsibilities or specialized legal counsel to assist with data breach obligations).

We will conduct a follow-up exercise within six months to allow time to remediate the key findings.

INDEX

communication tips *(continued)*
    practicing cultural awareness,
        100–101
    setting up backchannels, 96–97
Computer Security Incident Handling Guide
    (NIST SP 800-61r2), 19, 111
conference rooms, 38–39, 94–95
confidentiality, 45–46
confirmed compromises, 20
containment procedures, 14, 19
contracts, 11
conversation hogs, managing, 97–98
Cost of a Data Breach (Ponemon Institute
    and IBM Security), 7, 14
COVID-19 pandemic, 17
credit cards, 11
cross-training, 47
cryptocurrency mining, 15
cultural awareness, 100–101
cyber insurance, 48, 58, 113–114
Cybersecurity and Infrastructure
    Security Agency, 13–14, 58
cybersecurity tabletop exercises, xix

D

dark web data discovery example,
    138–141
data breaches, 7
    confirmed vs. suspected, 20
    financial impact of, 6–7
    notification requirements,
        20–21
    temporal requirements, 20
Data Protection Act, 6
date and time, choosing, 37–38
DDoS attacks, 16, 141–143
debrief, performing, 105–106
Defense Federal Acquisition
    Regulation Supplement
    (DFARS), 10, 11
Department of Health and Human
    Services, 20
Department of Homeland Security, xxii
development lead, 33–34
development team, 33–36, 43–44,
    103–104, 107, 112, 113
    evaluator, 36
    facilitator, 34

    lead, 33–34
    observer, 35
    subject matter expert, 34–35
    trusted agent, 35
discussion session, 43–44
distributed denial-of-service (DDoS)
    attacks, 16, 141–143
documentation, cataloging and
    updating, 112
DoD (Department of Defense), 11
duration, determining, 37

E

eBay, 16
email notification, 42–43
encouraging participation, 76–77
ENISA (European Union Agency for
    Cybersecurity), 14, 16, 110
escalation of threats, 8
escalation pace, scenario, 67–68
ethical responsibility, 21
etiquette for tabletop exercise, 75
European Union Agency for
    Cybersecurity, 14, 16, 110
evaluation methods, 105–107
    performing a debrief, 105
    sending a survey, 106–107
evaluation requirements, 103–104
evaluation restrictions, 104
evaluator, choosing an, 104–105
examining a recent cybersecurity
    incident, 12
executive audience, 135
executive checkpoint, 41–42
executive sponsor, 24, 41–43, 53, 96,
    101, 105, 107, 108, 113–114
    responsibilities for, 25–26
    selecting, 24
executive tabletop exercises, 9, 135
    dark web data discovery example,
        138–141
    DDoS attack example, 141–143
    ransomware example, 136–138
external facilitator, 47
external party notifications, 19
external sites, 39–40
external stakeholders, 48, 113
external vendors, 30

security incidents, preparing senior
leadership for, 9–10
security operations center (SOC), 30, 47
senior attendees, 97
senior-level exercises, 28–29
sensitive topics, 101
Shamoon virus, 16
smishing, 17
social distancing, 39
social media, 13
social media compromise example,
148–152
Sony Pictures, 16
stakeholders, 4, 39
statement of completion, 107–108
template, 157–159
storyboard
designing, 63–67
examples, 65, 69
Stuxnet, 16
subject matter expert, 34–35
supply chain attack, 130
supply chain compromise example,
130–133
surveys, sending, 106–107
suspected compromises, 20

T

tabletop exercises. *See also* advantages
of tabletop exercises; focus
areas; logistical considerations
defined, 3
educational component, 74
tactics for tabletop exercises, 88, 93–94
tandem exercises, 29
team responsibilities, 4
technical audience, 119
technical tabletop exercises, 9, 119
malware outbreak example,
126–130
phishing campaign example,
120–123
ransomware example, 123–126
supply chain compromise
example, 130–133

testing frequency, 19
third-party assessment, 48
threat landscape, 16
threats, identifying, 8
tools for tabletop exercises, 88
multimedia aids, 92–93
polling software, 88–91
recording devices and
software, 94
remote presentation software,
91–92
writing board, 88
tone, setting the, 40–41
topic, choosing a, 52–53
conferring with executive
sponsor, 53
consulting business impact
analysis, 52
leveraging other resources, 53
trend analysis, 114
trusted agent, 35, 96–97

U

US Department of Defense (DoD), 11
US Department of Health and Human
Services, 20
US Department of Homeland
Security, xxii
US Securities and Exchange
Commission (SEC), 9–10,
20, 59

V

vCISO (virtual chief information
security officer), 30, 47
vendor response, assessing, 27–28
vendors, working with, 30–32

W

working the room, 95–96
writing board, 88

Y

Yahoo, 16

Cybersecurity Tabletop Exercises is set in New Baskerville, Futura, and Dogma.

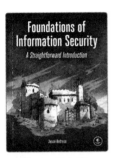

Never before has the world relied so heavily on the Internet to stay connected and informed. That makes the Electronic Frontier Foundation's mission—to ensure that technology supports freedom, justice, and innovation for all people—more urgent than ever.

For over 30 years, EFF has fought for tech users through activism, in the courts, and by developing software to overcome obstacles to your privacy, security, and free expression. This dedication empowers all of us through darkness. With your help we can navigate toward a brighter digital future.